facebook for
parents
answers to the top 25 questions

by **Linda Fogg Phillips** &
Dr. BJ Fogg, Stanford University

Captology Media
Stanford, California

Captology Media
Box 20456
Stanford, California 94309

ISBN 978-0-615-35473-6

Printed in the United States of America

Contents

What you should know about this book   1
What you should know about us   4

Facebook 101

1. Why do kids like Facebook so much?   7
2. Is Facebook just a fad?   11
3. Should I use Facebook?   15
4. How is Facebook changing our lives and our world?   21

Your child on Facebook

5. What is the #1 insight parents should have about Facebook?   27
6. Can I see who my kids are interacting with on Facebook?   31
7. How does Facebook change how kids communicate?   35
8. What age is too young for Facebook?   43
9. Is my teen's use of Facebook normal?   49

How Facebook privacy works (and doesn't work)

10. Why doesn't Facebook keep everything private?   53
11. Who can see what on Facebook?   57
12. How can I protect my child's privacy? Phase 1: Spring Cleaning   65
13. How can I protect my child's privacy? Phase 2: Settings   73
14. How can I protect my child's privacy? Phase 3: Daily Routine   87
15. What are the privacy loopholes on Facebook?   93
16. How can Facebook apps threaten privacy?   103

Protecting your family

17. How do I protect my child from strangers or unwanted friends?   107
18. How can I prevent bullying on Facebook?   111
19. Who owns the content posted to Facebook?   117
20. Can Facebook ruin my child's chances for a top college?   123

Best practices for parents

21. What if my kids won't friend me?   127
22. How do I fit in on Facebook?   131
23. How do I contact Facebook about a problem?   137
24. How do I stay current with Facebook?   143
25. How can I use Facebook as a parenting tool?   149

We welcome your feedback   159
Acknowledgments   161

What you should know about this book

Name:	Linda Fogg Phillips
Websites:	www.FacebookForParents.org

Name:	BJ Fogg
Websites:	http://bjfogg.com
	http://captology.stanford.edu

When we taught our first class on "Facebook for Parents" at Stanford University, we were surprised at the turnout. Hundreds of parents signed up to learn what their sons and daughters were doing on Facebook, and we couldn't fit everyone into our classroom. We realized parents needed a book.

Our goal in these pages is not to explain every Facebook feature. Instead, we focus on the 25 topics most relevant to parents whose kids use Facebook. If you scan the table of contents, you'll see those topics.

If parents don't understand Facebook, they won't know what their kids are doing for a good part of each day. Most parents wouldn't send their kids to a neighborhood they don't know, and Facebook is a vast neighborhood with its own rules. The more you learn, the more you'll see the pitfalls and potentials for your child on Facebook. This book will guide you.

We are a sister-brother team, and we wrote this book together. Linda is a mother of eight, who has seen Facebook influence teens at all stages. BJ is a Stanford research psychologist who specializes in how technology changes behavior. In this book, we put our heads together to make Facebook accessible to parents.

First of all, we've tailored the content for you. We learned what mattered to the 65 parents in our class at Stanford. And we did more research. At our website www.FacebookForParents.org we asked parents to tell us which topics mattered most to them. We received 3,681 responses from around the world.

We then selected the most important questions for this book. In the pages that follow, we answer those questions one by one.

We know you're busy. You're a parent. You may be reading our book while at the doctor's office or during your daughter's soccer game. In five minutes you can read most any chapter.

You can read chapters in any order. For example, if Question 12 interests you right now, you can skip ahead to that topic. Or if you are already using Facebook, the first section of this book—Facebook 101—may be too basic for you. It's okay to skim these early chapters or skip ahead to Section 2.

We kept the book short, clear, and small enough to fit in your purse or pack. Frankly, this is the kind of book we'd want to read: direct, efficient, and convenient.

To be clear, this is a book about Facebook for parents, not a book about parenting. We don't dictate how you should raise your children or how to run your household. Instead, we want you to see how Facebook is a new tool for parenting, hoping you'll apply your own parenting values in this new online world.

Don't worry if you do not have any experience with Facebook. This book will orient you. On the other hand, if you're already a Facebook expert, this book will help you learn more.

Facebook changes quickly. For example, the company often modifies the interface, and sometimes the privacy options change. To deal with this reality, we've created online videos for some of the topics. For example, in our chapters about privacy, we point you to online videos that we update to stay current with Facebook's changes. In our teaching, we were surprised at how much parents appreciated these short videos we made. So check them out and see for yourself.

To be clear, we don't have stock in Facebook or any financial interest in the company. We are fans of Facebook, but we're also critics. When there are things we don't like about Facebook, we'll tell you. But overall, we both agree that Facebook has enriched our lives, both personally and professionally.

On a larger scale, Facebook has changed the lives of millions, connecting friends over distances, bringing together parents and children after a fight, opening doors to new jobs, and helping people have empathy for other cultures. We won't tell all these stories in this book. We'll save that for the future. More urgent is helping you, right now, to start seeing Facebook as part of your child's life—and your own.

—Linda Fogg Phillips & BJ Fogg, Ph.D.

What you should know about us

| Name: | **Linda Fogg Phillips** |
| Websites: | **www.FacebookForParents.org** |

As the mother of eight children, ages 11 to 26, Linda Fogg Phillips brings a wealth of experience to *Facebook for Parents*. From her vantage point as a mother of active teens online, she has seen both the good and bad that Facebook can introduce into the life of a family.

Linda earned her Bachelor's Degree in Business from BYU. She has put this degree to use. In addition to her parenting responsibilities, she owns and operates a 16-horse boarding facility in Las Vegas that specializes in dressage and hunter/jumper horses.

Linda is involved, along with her husband and children, in CHOICE Humanitarian, a charitable organization that promotes sustainable development and micro-enterprise in countries with pressing needs. As a member of the Board of Directors, Linda oversees humanitarian projects in Guatemala.

(Linda is BJ's older sister.)

Name:	BJ Fogg
Websites:	http://bjfogg.com
	http://captology.stanford.edu

An experimental psychologist, Dr. BJ Fogg is the Director of Stanford's Persuasive Technology Lab. In his research and teaching, he helps people think clearly about behavior change in order to achieve real-world outcomes. The students in BJ's 2007 Facebook course created apps that motivated over 16 million user installations in 10 weeks.

In addition to his role at Stanford, BJ leads innovation projects for organizations in Silicon Valley and beyond. He holds nine patents, and he is the author or editor of five books. *Fortune Magazine* named him one of "10 New Gurus You Should Know."

BJ's life work is to shape technology innovation in ways that benefit the world and make people happier. He believes two principles are essential for achieving these goals: designing for simplicity and building relationships of trust. You can find more about him at www.bjfogg.com.

(BJ is Linda's younger brother.)

Why do kids like Facebook so much?

| Name: | Linda Fogg Phillips |
| Websites: | www.FacebookForParents.org |

What's so exciting to kids about Facebook?

After you spend some time "friending" your real-life friends on Facebook, you'll soon have your own answer. You'll see that Facebook is compelling to teens because it helps them keep up on the latest with their friends. They can share photos, chat together, and post little updates about their lives. They can play games with each other for free. Above all, they can engage their peers and get constant feedback, for better or worse. Most teens view Facebook as the one place where all their friends hang out, and it's the one place where all their potential friends are just waiting to be discovered.[1]

Kristi, one of the young adults on our Facebook for Parents Advisory Council, puts it this way:

"With Facebook, there is always a party going on at anytime where you can find and communicate with your friends, and the best part is that you can show up in your pajamas and nobody knows it."

Chris, a fourteen-year-old from Indianapolis explained that:

"Peer pressure plays a great role in why most people join Facebook. For me, that was the reason I joined in the first place. When people move or change schools they search for a way to stay together with the people who mean something to them, and this is an easy and popular way to do that."

He went on to say:

"Teens like Facebook because it is a great way to stay connected with friends and family when you can't stay connected with each other any other way."

Another member of our Facebook for Parents Advisory Council added her view:

"Facebook is a quicker and faster way to update friends that I don't see often because we live in different states or have different schedules. And this way, I'm not constantly being bombarded with people who I like to keep at a distance. Facebook allows me to keep the people I want in my inner circle in, and the people who are close acquaintances updated."

Some kids feel that Facebook allows them to build stronger and more meaningful friendships because they can connect with multiple friends more easily than with other methods. This was evident in the comment made by Leavitt:

"Facebook eliminates the awkward part of the conversation when the other person says, 'So . . . tell me what you've been up to?' I already know, and I can ask more deep-thought provoking questions like, 'I saw your photos from England; tell me more about it.' I can be more specific and ask questions."

I wouldn't worry that your child will become a Facebook hermit who uses Facebook relationships to replace real relationships. In the cases we've seen, kids use Facebook mostly to build on existing real-life relationships.

In the first Facebook class that BJ taught at Stanford back in 2007, he studied his 84 students to determine why they were drawn to Facebook. Overall, students saw Facebook as a convenient and respectable way to connect socially. More specifically, the results revealed that his students used Facebook to:

1. Feel connected to existing friends
2. Stay updated on existing friends
3. Get information about new people
4. Start and build relationships
5. Express their identity and views

Since then, as we examine related research, we've found these five motives apply to teens and adults equally. That's not so surprising. As humans, we are hardwired to connect with other humans. Belonging is one of our deepest needs. And teens today are figuring out how to fill this need, with Facebook as their primary tool.

"I don't have time to call all of my friends every day," says Ashley, a seventeen-year-old senior, "but I can get on Facebook and see what they have been doing and make comments. With my busy life of school, homework, sports and a job, Facebook helps me stay involved with more of my friends than I would be able to otherwise."

Ashley goes on to admit that Facebook is the last thing she does at night and the first thing she does in the morning before heading out to school. She also logs on periodically throughout the day. Is this typical of most kids? It depends on the kid. Is this a "soft addiction"? Perhaps. As a parent you need to determine if

Facebook use is interfering with your child's life.

A parent approached me with a concern that her fifteen-year-old daughter's grades had dropped from A's to C's since she became involved with Facebook. She felt that Kara was indeed addicted to Facebook. After some lengthy discussions with her parents, Kara agreed to take a "Facebook vacation" until her grades recovered—not an easy decision for Kara, but the alternative was worse. As you can see in the post below, Kara announced her hiatus and her mother gave her a "virtual high five."

Is Facebook addicting to adults? It can be!

For the parents who took our first class at Stanford, this was one of the biggest surprises. They actually enjoyed using Facebook. Many expressed what a "time suck" it was becoming in their lives, as they were enticed to use Facebook more and more. In fact, some admitted that they started to love using Facebook, just like their teenage children. Overall, the parents became less worried about their kids on Facebook and more interested in how Facebook made their own lives more interesting.

References

1 Adam Joinson, 2008. "Looking at, Looking up or Keeping up with People? Motives and Use of Facebook," Proceedings of the 26th Annual SIGCHI conference on Human Factors in Computing Systems, (2008): 1027-1036. http://doi.acm.org/10.1145/1357054.1357213.

Is Facebook just a fad?

Name: **BJ Fogg**
Websites: **http://bjfogg.com**
http://captology.stanford.edu

From Pet Rocks to leg warmers, we've all seen fads come and go. So with Facebook's soaring popularity, it's fair to ask, "Is Facebook just another fad?"

We say no. Facebook is not merely a fashion of the moment. Instead, Facebook is more like the mobile phone. It's an innovation that makes our lives easier and better. Most who start using Facebook don't give it up, because the rewards far outweigh the risks. Facebook is here to stay.

Millions of us have made Facebook a routine part of our daily lives. We post photos, share details about our days, and wish friends happy birthday, all through one service. What we're doing on Facebook today—using our true identities to connect and share with others online—has become part of our culture.

In fact, if Facebook, Inc., fumbles at some point, another company will quickly pick up the ball and run. But Linda and I think fumbling by Facebook is unlikely. In fact, we think Facebook has already won the social networking game. No previous company has ever attracted over 500,000 new users each day for an entire year. That's what Facebook has achieved, and the growth is not yet slowing down. This makes it all the more important to learn about Facebook today.

Our children will use social networking for the rest of their lives, with friends, classmates, and work colleagues. And it's not just our children. We predict that if you, as a parent, are not yet using Facebook, you will eventually. We've seen this over and over: Despite firm intentions to never join Facebook, people are eventually won over. When enough friends and family members talk about what they shared on Facebook, resisters start to feel left out, and the temptation to try it becomes overwhelming. Soon people see why Facebook is so fun.

That's when people understand why the business world has also bought deeply into Facebook. It's not just another web site; it is now a platform for companies to reach people. Thousands of brands—including American Express and Proctor and Gamble— are investing time and energy into using Facebook. Startup companies spent hundreds of millions of dollars in the last year alone to deliver their services through Facebook. This makes Facebook essential to their success, and they do not want Facebook to go away any time soon.

The initial social networking services, from The Well to Friendster, arrived on the scene too early. Not enough people were online to reach critical mass. Facebook got started at just the right time in history, a point where both children and grandparents were becoming comfortable using the web. When Facebook launched in 2004, going online wasn't just for geeks any more.

Some have said that Facebook is getting stale and that people are leaving. Journalists like to write this story, but the facts simply don't support this view. Facebook is growing; few people are leaving. And the time people spend on Facebook grows larger.

Facebook is here to stay for as far as we can see into the future. If the company behind Facebook happens to stumble and fall—and again, we think they will not—a similar service (perhaps from Google) will take the lead.

The social networking we're doing today is certainly not a fad. It's a shift in our lives as permanent as the mobile phone. The sooner we understand how Facebook works, the better we can learn how to best use Facebook to enrich our lives, and—perhaps more critical to parents—the better we can protect our families from the potential negative effects of living in this brave new world.

So let's get started.

Should I use Facebook?

Name:	**Linda Fogg Phillips**
Websites:	**www.FacebookForParents.org**

In my life before Facebook, I thought I knew my kids—their concerns, their opinions, and their friends. We had created a home where our kids could be themselves, and where their friends were always welcome to hang out. At dinnertime we often had young guests sitting around our table, in addition to our family of ten. By listening to the lively chatter, my husband and I learned a lot about their lives.

For about a year, my brother BJ had been suggesting that I get a Facebook account. But I didn't see the need. After all, it's a thing for teens and college kids anyway—right? Facebook was not for me. Besides, I had time only for those things most vital to being a mom. And Facebook, I thought, was not vital.

I remember the exact moment when I realized how wrong I had been.

It was Thanksgiving. My extended family came to my home for the holiday, and BJ and I were in the kitchen peeling potatoes and catching up. If you had been there with us, you would have seen my surprised face when BJ said, "I see that Amber has a new boyfriend."

"A new boyfriend!" I thought. I didn't even know that she had an old boyfriend.

"Really?" I said. "Did she tell you that?"

"No, she didn't tell me," BJ said. "I saw it on Facebook."

Reality hit me in the face like a bucket of ice water. My kids were living in a world I didn't know, a world I'd chosen to ignore. As a mom, that was not what I wanted.

I was quiet, but my mind was racing.

"Okay" I said, pointing my potato peeler at BJ. "I'm ready to join Facebook. Tell me what I need to do."

Later that afternoon I started my journey into an unfamiliar world. It was a bit scary. Fortunately, I had one of the world's Facebook experts to help me, my own brother.

I would soon see how Facebook can bring families together. As the months went by I experienced how vital Facebook is in the life of today's parent. I got more connected with my kids' concerns, their opinions, and their friends—more than ever before. I could no longer imagine a mom's life without Facebook.

Yes, it was a big shift. I had once rejected Facebook as "not for me." But with time, experience, and deeper insight, I would later embrace Facebook as the "Power Tool of Parenting."

Should you use Facebook? My overall answer is yes. But I'll get to that later. Let me first point out why you may want to avoid Facebook. I see five drawbacks.

Drawback #1: Your info will get shared widely

If you use Facebook, your personal information will get shared with others. Usually you share with people you select as Friends. But like it or not, some of your information will get shared widely (See Question 11 for details). The current design of Facebook makes it impossible to use this service and stay invisible to the world.

In Questions 12 and 13 we explain how to share your content wisely. But despite this instruction, at some point you'll probably drop your guard. For example, you may post a photo on Facebook and forget to restrict who can view it. As a result, almost anyone will be able see your photo until you change the privacy settings.

Employers, banks, and the IRS have found Facebook to be a helpful way to learn about people. An attorney friend of mine explained that his firm often uses Facebook as a source of leads in building a case. You can minimize most risks if you follow what we explain later. But remember, you or your child might not take the right steps to guard your family's privacy.

Drawback #2: Your kids might get upset

If you join Facebook, your child might be upset—at least in the beginning. In our work with parents, we've seen this many times. A parent joins Facebook and the child feels threatened. The fact is that your presence on Facebook may create tension in your home, especially when you first start using the service. However, over time, as parents demonstrate their Facebook smarts, the kids seem to get over it.

Of course, not all kids get upset when their parents join Facebook. Even so, this is one issue that parents confront—and often fear. Yes, it's a drawback, but I don't think it should stop you from using Facebook.

Drawback #3: You might spend too much time online

As we teach parents about Facebook, we suggest they spend five minutes a day using the service. Everyone can find five minutes, right? But sometimes parents end up spending much longer. They get sucked into Facebook. The good news here is that parents finally understand why their kids find Facebook so compelling.

The bad news is that parents might spend a lot more time online than before. This may come at the expense of other priorities. You might start checking Facebook at work, and that could be a problem. Or you may find yourself spending Saturday nights on Facebook rather than out on the town with friends. Even worse, you may be hanging out on Facebook instead of talking with your children.

You know this fact, but I'll say it anyway: Facebook can be addicting.

Drawback #4: You might forget face-to-face conversations

Facebook is designed to be convenient. You log on when you want, and your Facebook Friends log on at their leisure. Online you interact mostly through text and photos. It gives the illusion that you're really connecting with people.

Because all this works so well on Facebook, you may find yourself replacing face-to-face conversations with Facebook interactions. This means you lose the richness of voice and the warmth of being physically present with people. The challenge is to resist letting Facebook replace what humans have done for thousands of years: meeting face to face and talking together in real time. Nothing beats that experience. Not even Facebook.

Drawback #5: You might embarrass yourself or your child

I've heard quite a few stories from grownups who have embarrassed themselves on Facebook. It happens to the best of us. For example, you might try to post a funny comment only to see it fall flat.

The potential for embarrassment extends beyond yourself to your children. If you embarrass your child, you confirm your child's worst fears about you being on Facebook. We want to help you avoid this. In later chapters we explain how you can steer clear of big mistakes, with Question 22 taking on this topic directly.

Yes, Facebook is for parents

Given these five drawbacks, you may figure you're better off forgetting about Facebook altogether. But you would be making a mistake. At least that's how I see it.

The question about using Facebook seems like questions we've faced before: "Should I use email?" and "Should I buy a mobile phone?" Perhaps you once struggled with these questions. But today the answers are obvious.

In earlier times, people probably wondered, "Should I buy a Model T or stick with my horse-drawn carriage?" Just as the automobile forever changed physical mobility in our society, Facebook is changing how we connect with each other, how we share our feelings, our ideas, and our lives. So unless you want to be left behind in a cloud of dust in your horse-drawn carriage, you should grab the steering wheel and learn to drive. It's the best thing for parents to do.

Kids naturally drift from their parents as they assert their independence. Facebook helps us stay connected to them. Even if your child doesn't want to friend you on Facebook, you can establish your own circle and experience what the Facebook fuss is all about. This alone will allow you to better understand the online world in which your child lives.

Today, your interest in Facebook may be mostly to protect your child, or to stay current with your child's technology use. Those are valid motivations. But if you're like the parents we've taught, I predict you have a surprise waiting—a good one. The more you learn about Facebook, the less anxious you'll be about your child, and the more fascinating you'll find this new frontier.

How is Facebook changing our lives and our world?

Name:	BJ Fogg
Websites:	http://bjfogg.com
	http://captology.stanford.edu

Facebook is changing our lives more than any other website or high-tech innovation. Most changes are good, benefiting us personally, socially, and globally. But some of what's changing isn't so pretty. Certainly one could write an entire book—or a series of books—about how Facebook affects our lives and our world, because this is a large and fascinating area. But like other chapters in our book, I will keep my answer brief.

As a social scientist I tend to view issues at different levels, ranging from internal to global. On the internal level, one might ask, "Is Facebook making us happier as individuals?" At the other extreme, the global level, one question might be, "Can Facebook make our world more peaceful?" I've written about both of those issues elsewhere. In this chapter I want to share new insights, and, true to my social scientist perspective, I will organize my response into levels of impact.

- Personal
- Interpersonal
- Social
- Cultural
- Global

Personal Impact: Always on stage

How is Facebook changing our personal lives? If you're active on Facebook, you probably have an answer to this question. But the impact on young lives is different. In fact, when I was teaching my "Psychology of Facebook" class at Stanford, one insight from my students surprised me. The students explained that because of Facebook, they were always being observed, always under scrutiny. As one student put it, she was "always on stage," even if she didn't want to be.

Imagine that you're a student at Stanford today. Whenever you are with your friends, you know a camera is also there, part of everyone's mobile phone. This means anything you do can be photographed, even without you knowing it. If your friend takes a picture of you, she naturally posts the image to Facebook. Once posted online and tagged (tagging is a way of indicating who is in the photo), the photo is visible to all your Facebook friends. This happens whether you like it or not. The overall result is this: What was once personal and private—such as hanging out in your dorm room with friends—is now potentially public and permanent.

When my students explained this dynamic to me, I was blown away. I couldn't imagine having such surveillance over my life as a teenager or a college student. Big Brother has arrived on campus, thanks to the combination of online social networks and camera-phones everywhere. As you can imagine, this is one of the ways Facebook has changed things for the worse, and in this regard, I feel sad for my students today. They are always on stage. What pressure this must create!

Interpersonal Impact: Friends don't disappear

The next level for understanding the impact of Facebook is the interpersonal level, how we interact with other individuals.

When you were growing up, you probably moved to a new school at some point and left old friends behind. Perhaps you tried to stay in touch via letters or phone calls. Usually the friendships faded, and perhaps even today you regret drifting from a good friend. At the same time, when you moved to a new place, you left behind people you didn't like so much. You were probably relieved to be rid of the bully who made your life harder.

Today with Facebook, moving to a new school or city doesn't affect relationships as much as when you were young. You can stay in touch with old friends better. But at the same time, the people you didn't like, such as the bully, are still connected to you. Even if you don't friend the bully on Facebook, perhaps one of your friends will, and this puts the bully into your Facebook experience from time to time.

For better or worse, Facebook connects us so well that friends don't disappear when we move to a new location or new phase of our lives.

Social Impact: Many relationships, fewer deep ones

Today, it's not unusual for teens and college students to have 800 or more friends on Facebook. I never had this many friends when I was young, and you probably didn't either. But most young people have a large network of people they call friends.

But what about true friends?

When you were growing up, your friendships were determined mostly by location: where you lived, and where you attended school or church. You probably had a handful of close friends and a few dozen good friends. And that was it. You didn't have 800 relationships to manage.

With 800 friends on Facebook, young people today sacrifice quality of friendship for quantity. The same is true for adults using Facebook. We all have limited energy to create and nurture relationships. With so many friends, we have less capacity to create deep, close friendships.

Cultural Impact: News & entertainment filtered through friends

For businesses, the most important impact Facebook and other social media creates is playing out at a cultural level.

More and more, our news about the world comes to us through friends, not through broadcast or print media. Our social network is a filter. This means that if no one in my social network cares about the water crisis in California, I may not learn about this issue. However, if my friends care deeply about education, I may get lots of info about that topic.

How does this work? When friends on Facebook post something, such as a news story about education, that link can appear in the News Feed on my Facebook Home Page. If I see something interesting in my News Feed, I click on it. In this case, I would click on the education story link, which may take me to a New York Times article. This is sort of like a friend bringing a news clipping to my house.

As we spend more time with Facebook and other social media, we spend less time reading newspapers or watching TV news. This means I will see fewer news stories that professional editors have chosen, and I will see more stories my friends think are important. The same is true for entertainment. I may not see a movie trailer on TV, but if my Facebook friend posts it on Facebook, I can watch it there.

And this is where businesses get grumpy. Since broadcast and print are getting weaker, they can't advertise as effectively in the old ways. They have to figure out how to reach us in new ways—such as Facebook and other social media. And this has given many big companies migraines. (Stay tuned. We've not yet seen the end to this drama.)

Global Impact: World without borders

The final level of impact is global. Around the world, hundreds of millions are using Facebook. So it's no surprise that Facebook is changing us at a global level. This change, more than any other, is one that excites me. I'm optimistic that Facebook is making our world a more peaceful and empathetic place. To see how much we've changed globally, consider the example that follows.

Imagine yourself back in tenth grade. It's Friday, and you're sitting in the classroom for social studies. Your teacher announces that you have an assignment due Monday. You need to find three people living in Europe to interview. You need to ask them about how health care works in their country. "Good luck," your teacher says. "See you on Monday!"

When I was in tenth grade, I would have little idea how to find three people in Europe to interview. With extreme efforts, my parents could probably arrange phone calls with an old friend in Germany and one distant relative in England. But this would come at a large cost of time and money.

Now let's fast forward to today. Imagine a tenth grader given the same assignment in school. What would she do? Well, she would likely turn to Facebook. In a few hours, she could complete the assignment and have it ready by Monday, without any parental involvement.

Today's tenth grader sees the world differently than we saw things at that age. They likely have friends from many countries, and they are probably better at seeing the world from others' perspectives. Facebook and other social media are creating a world without borders.

As these young people grow up and become the leaders of our cities, states, and countries, they will bring with them that global perspective. When conflicts arise, they will be better equipped to resolve them. At some point, we will have leaders around the world who all grew up using Facebook and other social media as kids.

Why Facebook matters

Even though Facebook changes our lives in some negative ways, overall I'm optimistic that Facebook and other social media are changing our world for the better. As we learn to share and connect through the Internet for fun—sharing photos, movies, games—we also expand our ability to use these same channels for serious work, like containing epidemic flu or resolving international conflicts. To solve the problems we face today and in the future, we will need powerful collaboration tools and people who know how to use them well. And for me, that's why Facebook matters.

What is the #1 insight for parents about Facebook?

Name:	Linda Fogg Phillips
Websites:	www.FacebookForParents.org

Does the idea of monitoring your child's behavior on Facebook make you feel guilty? Do you worry about barging in on your child's private world? If so, you are not alone. I've found that many parents see Facebook as a private space for their child, like a bedroom or a personal diary.

We faced this issue early in our teaching. After our first class session at Stanford, a woman came up to talk with me in private.

"Thanks for offering this class," she said. "But I have to admit I feel a bit guilty using Facebook, like I'm intruding on my daughter's private space."

The woman explained her policy: She doesn't snoop in her daughter's bedroom, looking in drawers or in journals. She doesn't monitor her phone calls or text messages. They have an agreement.

"It feels like I'm crossing the line with Facebook," she said.

"Trust me," I said. "There's nothing private about Facebook."

When our next class arrived, BJ and I had a better answer for this woman, and every parent in class. "Facebook," we said, "is not like a private bedroom. The best metaphor for Facebook is your front lawn."

As we explained this "front lawn" idea, we saw relief come to parents' faces. They somehow knew the "private bedroom" idea was not quite right. But when kids argued that Facebook was their private space, like a bedroom, parents were at a loss. Now, our students had a new way to think about Facebook. The front lawn made sense.

As we continued to share this idea, the response from parents in our classes and workshops has led us to conclude that this insight—Facebook as Front Lawn—is the #1 thing parents should know about Facebook. If you take this perspective, you will have better intuition about how your family should use (or not use) this service. You'll be able to apply your own parenting values to know what is appropriate for your family on Facebook.

To help you explain the Front Lawn idea to your spouse or child, I will start by debunking "Facebook as Bedroom."

Three reasons Facebook is not like a bedroom

First of all, strangers don't enter a child's bedroom. But on Facebook, your child can interact with strangers. And sometimes strangers will view your child's comments and information, and you have no control over that.

Next, the activities in a bedroom are not observable by hundreds of people. In contrast, what your child does on Facebook is widely observable.

Finally, what goes on in a bedroom is not recorded, potentially forever. In contrast, what happens on Facebook can be recorded and stored, not just by Facebook, Inc., but by many people who have permission to observe you.

Why front lawn is the right metaphor

Now consider why the "front lawn" metaphor is more accurate. First, strangers might step onto your front lawn; they might knock on your door. That's not so unusual. And yes, that's how Facebook works too.

Next, what happens on your front lawn is observable, just like acts on Facebook. For example, if you have a party on your front lawn, it's visible to neighbors and people passing by. If your family has an argument on the front lawn, that's also observable by outsiders. And that's what happens with arguments on Facebook: People can see all the action, play by play.

And finally, what happens on your front lawn can be recorded and stored by anyone who can observe. A snoopy neighbor may be recording your party with a hidden video camera. Or if you are arguing on your front lawn, someone within earshot could take notes. In a similar way, these recording and storage issues are true for most Facebook activities.

In other words, as your child does things on Facebook—posting photos, interacting with people, announcing emotions—think about those things happening on your front lawn, not in a private bedroom.

Applying the front lawn metaphor

Certainly, in today's world there are things you wouldn't want your child doing on your front lawn. There are people you don't want hanging out on your front lawn. You can apply this metaphor to how your family uses Facebook. Consider these questions, for example.

- *Can your child hang out with strangers on your front lawn?*
- *Should you feel guilty about wanting to be on your front lawn with your child?*
- *Can your child post provocative photos on your front lawn?*

We won't answer the above questions for you, since these decisions hinge on your parenting style. Some parents may be quite restrictive about what happens on their front lawn; it's part of the home, and it affects the family reputation. Other parents may be more permissive.

Whatever your parenting style, Facebook has nothing to do with a private bedroom. A Facebook account presents a public and potentially permanent face for all to see. So when your teen says what she does on Facebook is her private business, you might say, "Facebook is not your private bedroom. Facebook is like our front lawn. What you post on Facebook is family business."

Once this idea is established with your family, when future Facebook issues arise with your child (and they likely will), you can explain your position by saying two little words: "Front Lawn."

Can I see who my kids are interacting with on Facebook?

Name:	Linda Fogg Phillips
Websites:	www.FacebookForParents.org

The simple answer to that question is yes, you can see who your kids are interacting with on Facebook. That is, if you are their Facebook Friend. If you are not their Facebook Friend, then it gets a bit more complicated, but the answer is still yes. Remember, Facebook is a public forum where almost everything posted is visible to friend or foe in one way or another. Hopefully as a parent you fall into the "friend" category and not the "foe."

Let me share with you an instance when one of my children placed me in the "foe" category and removed me as one of her Facebook Friends. Once I was not her Friend on Facebook, it was much more difficult to know who she was interacting with online. I was blocked from viewing all of her Facebook activities.

One evening as I signed onto Facebook, I saw in my News Feed that one of my daughters had been "tagged" in some photos. Naturally, I was interested and took a look at them, noticing other people who had been tagged in the photos and reading the comments.

"Hmmm. Come take a look at these photos on Facebook," I said to my husband.

"You are always on Facebook!" he exclaimed as he approached and leaned over my computer. When he saw what I had discovered, he asked with disgust, "Where did those pictures come from? Who took them, and where are they? Why is she hanging out with those friends?"

"Hang on, hang on. Those are a lot of questions that I don't have the answers to."

"She needs to be grounded for a month!"

"Wait, honey, let's talk about how we want to handle this. Facebook relationships are delicate—"

Unfortunately, my daughter came walking into the room at that very moment. She caught us in mid-sentence and could tell that she had interrupted a "discussion."

Once confronted, she froze with a puzzled look on her face. I'm sure she was thinking "Okay, who told on me?" I didn't want her to know Facebook was the source.

Not wanting to get into trouble, she immediately went into some weak explanation about the night before. But we didn't buy it.

My husband jumped into the fray, citing the evidence like a lawyer in a courtroom. "Mom saw the pictures on Facebook!" he announced, motioning to me still sitting at my computer.

My daughter glared at me with a sense of betrayal. She marched up the stairs and into her room.

"Thanks honey! Just throw me under the bus!"

Why did my daughter post a photo she knew would get her into trouble? She didn't. Her friend posted the photo, and the Facebook system put a notice in my Feed. That's how all this started.

The next day when I checked my Facebook account, I was not only removed as one of her Friends, but I was blocked as well! I could not even find her in a search. She had vanished from my Facebook world.

Great! We had discovered one act of disobedience, but now I had lost one of my key parenting tools. At that point, I would not be able to see her activities on Facebook directly. I would have to ask a mutual Friend to update me on my daughter. Or I could ask one of my other children to do so. Neither was ideal.

There is always a silver lining to instances such as this. My daughter's act of blocking me helped me realize that I needed to strengthen my relationship with that particular daughter, and I made the effort to do so. In a short period of time, I was back on her Friends List—both on Facebook and in life.

By creating positive interactions on Facebook, we earn the respect to discipline our children when necessary, but we must use discretion or our teens will find ways to block us.

Keep in mind that kids often think that the only reason parents want to friend them on Facebook is to "spy" on them, so proceed with caution here. Facebook is a useful parenting tool that assists us in being more in touch with the thoughts, actions and friends of our children, but it is also a tool not to be misused.

We build a positive Facebook relationship with our children much the same way we do in the real world. We have to make our presence in our children's Facebook lives a rewarding experience for them. If our children enjoy our presence in their virtual world, they won't block us or create secret accounts. This keeps the window open for us to see who our children are interacting with in the Facebook community and in their real-world community as well.

I connect with my kids in a positive way when I write on their Walls something like: "Congratulations on your first place at the swim meet today, Nicole! Keep up the hard work!" Many of her Facebook Friends will add their congratulations.

Or when my son is out of town, I may update my status to read: "My house is so quiet when Brandon is gone. I miss him!" Many of our mutual Friends will comment.

I will often send a private message to my children on Facebook, such as "I love you" or "thanks for doing such a great job cleaning your room."

These are ways that I strengthen my ties with my children. This also helps maintain my ability to see who they are interacting with on Facebook.

Now that I'm a Facebook mom, I can't imagine parenting without employing Facebook as another window into my children's lives and into who their friends are. When a parent tells me, "I don't want to bother with Facebook," it's as if they are saying "I don't care who my kids are interacting with online." Through Facebook, I'm as engaged with what's going on in my children's online social lives as I am in what's going on with their education or real world lives.

The bottom line is this: If you are Friends with your children on Facebook, use discretion with the information that you gather, and respect their boundaries. You want them to enjoy your presence in their Facebook lives.

How does Facebook change how kids communicate?

Name:	**BJ Fogg**	
Websites:	**http://bjfogg.com**	
	http://captology.stanford.edu	

If you're lucky, on your next birthday you'll wake up in Hawaii, ready to enjoy a carefree day on the beach with your spouse. After a morning walk, let's suppose you return to your beach house and log onto Facebook. You see posted on your Facebook Wall a message from your daughter: "Happy bday. Love you <3 !" This little note makes you feel good.

As the day goes on, you are hoping for something more from your daughter. A phone call, at least. Perhaps she sent a card along with your spouse, and your spouse will present it to you at dinner! As the sun sets on your birthday, you realize that none of these things are going to happen. Your daughter, who loves you, has used a Wall Post on Facebook to share her feelings on your birthday.

Maybe the Hawaii story hasn't happened to you yet. But if you start using Facebook, some version of it probably will. Now that Facebook has conquered much of our written communications, your child will reach out in a way that won't seem very fitting to you. Linda and I are on your side, but frankly, there's not much any of us can do to change this trend, any more than you can convince your child to wear your old bell bottom jeans.

The new digital technologies, especially texting and Facebook, have revolutionized how kids communicate. As I step back to make sense of the changes, I see three trends emerging. The first is most obvious: The channels teens use today are different from what you and I used at that age. Second, a sense of what's private seems to be evaporating. Compared to our Boomer generation, teens are more comfortable with just putting everything out there, warts and all, for anyone to see. Finally, the way teens communicate seems shallower, with less emotional richness. Let's start with the first trend: channels.

Trend #1: New channels for communicating

Many channels that you and I used to communicate as teens are dying, if not dead already. Remember the handwritten letter? How about the thank-you note? If your child has affixed a stamp to a letter in the last year, congratulations. This expressive way to share your thoughts and feelings with an intimate has become rare in today's world.

Even email is passé among teens. This surprises some parents, but the evidence shows that teens use email as an old-fashioned way to communicate with adults and institutions.[1] Teens don't email each other. That would be uncool. Instead, teens text each other. Or they use Facebook.

But Facebook isn't just one channel. It is many. Through Facebook, users can send "Private Messages," which is similar to email. And they can "Chat," which is instant messaging. One very popular way to communicate on Facebook is by posting on somebody's Wall. Each person on Facebook has their own Wall. You can think of the Wall as a bulletin board attached to a dorm room door.

As friends pass by, they can write a little note, post a picture, or just browse through what's already posted.

Consider this example: Greg posts a note on Marsha's Wall. Everyone can see it. To respond, Marsha posts something on Greg's Wall. Back and forth it goes, and anyone can join in or quietly observe. Over time, this creates a conversation that lasts days or weeks.

Wall postings became so popular that Facebook redesigned its interface to make the Wall more prominent. They also added a feature called "Wall to Wall," which makes following the discussion easier.

A popular channel on Facebook is photo sharing, which includes commenting on photos. These comments matter. If a photo doesn't get comments, it's pretty much a failure. Comments are the secret sauce of social media. To post a photo and start a cascade of comments—now that's success.

The last Facebook channel of note is Status Messages. This is perhaps the most prominent feature of Facebook. When you log in, you see a bit of white space, eager to be filled. The Status Message is like a bumper sticker you attach to your Facebook identity. When you update again, you add another sticker to your profile. People use Status Messages in many ways, from celebration to mourning, from statements to questions.

The Status Message helps teens express their identity. As a parent, you'll learn a lot about your child by reading their Status Messages carefully.

Much of what I've explained so far I've said as a social scientist who tracks these trends. The next two trends are harder to quantify, yet they seem just as important.

Trend #2: Decorum is dying

Ugh. I hate to use the word "decorum" in my writing; it sounds so old-fashioned. But the way I see young people hash out private matters publicly on Facebook makes me think no other word expresses what teens seem to have lost. Consider this example: One of my students uses the Wall to invite women on dates. Remember: The Wall is public. That's an aggressive move, if you ask me. Or consider the sad updates some young people post: "I'm such a loser." These messages seem like desperate cries for help broadcast to anyone who will listen.

The lack of decorum extends to racy images posted for all to see, as well as the language teens use in Comments and Status Messages. Even Stanford students will, at times, use four-letter words and phrases I don't hear them say in my classroom. Consider the acronym "FML" (if you don't know what FML means, try Google). Data from 2009 revealed that "FML" was among the most commonly posted items on Facebook status updates.[2]

At first, all this emotion in such a short, public package can be bewildering to parents and teachers. But over time, when you see enough of this stuff on Facebook, the novelty wears off and becomes a sea of banality. What was once whispered to confidants is now shouted through Facebook's megaphone for anyone to hear.

I suspect your child sees everyone else sharing in public what might better be left in private. To teens, this probably appears to be normal behavior. The culture has shifted, and frankly, there's nothing we can do to change this trend.

But there may be a silver lining. Consider the Profile Pictures young people upload to Facebook. These aren't always the images I would choose for them. In fact, at times I'm still surprised by the photos I see my Stanford students select to represent themselves on Facebook. It almost seems that the less flattering the mugshot, the better.

When I see a less-than-perfect profile picture on Facebook, part of me wonders: Maybe the death of decorum is actually a good thing. Let me explain.

Today, thanks to the culture of Facebook, teens seem to be honestly sharing how they feel. And they know it's okay to be less than perfect. They see their friends' foibles all the time on Facebook. That's quite a different world than some of us grew up with in the "Dress for Success" eighties and the "Brand You" nineties.

With online social networks, anytime of the day or night, young people can share their emotions. And usually friends respond quickly. Granted, it may be just a brief comment on Facebook, but still, someone has heard them. The comments offer support and commiseration. That can't be all bad. In fact, the long-term impact of this trend might be very good.

Trend #3: Convenience over depth

This third trend probably won't surprise you. Teens today often choose to communicate in the easiest way, even if this sacrifices depth and richness. For example, a phone conversation conveys a lot of information, thanks to tone of voice and how miraculous humans are with language.

In contrast, with texting it's difficult to convey a nuanced thought. Yet texting is often more convenient. I probably don't have to tell you which channel teens prefer most on their mobiles. Research confirms what many parents see each day: U.S. teens use their phones more for texting than for voice calls.[3]

This might be fine if such quick messages added a deeper dimension to our traditional means of connecting, but the new channels can trump other forms. With a mobile phone always a factor, at any instant your teen may flee into a text message, putting your face-to-face conversation on hold.

Teens do not pen long letters to grandma, or to anyone for that matter. Those days are gone. But you might think that maybe—just maybe—your teenager would send a "thank you" card to grandma, writing a little note and putting it in postal mail. This gives grandma a moment of happiness, as well as a tangible keepsake. From what I can tell, that old ritual is rare. If grandma is lucky, and if she's on Facebook, she's likely to get a Wall Post: "Hey, thanks for the birthday present." And with that quick note, the modern "thank you" ritual has been performed.

I don't think we, as Boomers or parents, can change these trends. We are better off learning to surf the wave rather than getting wiped out by it. Suppose your daughter is upstairs in the den on the computer, and you want her to come to dinner. You may prefer sending her a chat message on Facebook rather than yelling up the stairs. Just type a few words into Facebook and you know your message gets delivered.

As a social scientist, I've studied close relationships—how they form and how they enrich our lives. So I'm never going to be satisfied with mere text messages or Facebook Wall Posts. Face-to-face conversations matter. Using our voices to express ideas and emotions is nothing short of miraculous.

But the convenience of texting, chat, and Wall Posts can serve a purpose. These channels can keep us connected to people when other channels don't work. In other words, the lightweight connectivity of texting or on Facebook can keep the door open to deeper, richer interactions with those people who matter most. For parents the implication seems clear: If you don't keep the door open by using the channels teens love, you will miss many opportunities to connect with your teen in deeper ways.

1 "Teens and Technology" by Amanda Lenhart, Paul Hitlin, Mary Madden. Pew Internet & American Life Project, 2005. See www.pewinternet.org

2 http://blog.facebook.com/blog.php?post=215076352130

3 "Teens and Sexting" by Amanda Lenhart. Pew Internet & American Life Project, 2009. See www.pewinternet.org

What age is too young for Facebook?

facebook

Name: **Linda Fogg Phillips**
Websites: **www.FacebookForParents.org**

A reporter from *The New York Times* phoned me and asked me to answer a reader's question about his eleven-year-old using Facebook: "What age is too young for Facebook?"

My family often talks about Facebook at the dinner table. Their feedback helps me see Facebook in new ways. For this reader's question, I figured I'd better consult an authority. I turned to my eleven-year-old daughter, Summer.

"So Summer, what is the youngest age that you think is appropriate for a Facebook account?" I asked.

"Twelve," she stated without hesitation.

"Twelve? Why twelve?"

"Cause sometimes ten-year-olds do stupid things, and eleven is pretty close to ten. So I think it should be twelve."

My mind flashed back to a few months earlier when this same eleven-year-old daughter begged me to allow her to open her own account even though she knew that she did not meet Facebook's minimum age requirement of thirteen.

"Please, mom, please," she had pleaded. "I'm the only one in the family who isn't on Facebook."

This was true simply because she is the youngest child. (Oh, wait a minute, let me back up here. Summer wasn't the only family member without a Facebook account. My husband did not have one either, but that's a different story.)

"I feel left out," she said, blinking her big eyes for effect. "I want to talk to Nana and Papa on Facebook, too." (Now she was playing the sympathy card. She expected me to fall for that?)

Back at the dinner table . . .

"So McCall, what do you think?" I asked my thirteen-year-old.

Two years previously, McCall had added sixteen years to her age without my knowledge by telling Facebook that she was born in 1980 instead of 1996. This is how some underage kids start their accounts. To outsiders, it must have seemed odd that a twenty-seven-year-old had so much interest in boy bands and so many teenage friends. No Facebook authority noticed anything wrong, but then her mother became Facebook-savvy.

"I think twelve is a good age," she agreed.

"But McCall, you had an account at eleven. Why?"

"Because you wouldn't let me have a MySpace."

Hmmm. I hadn't given permission for Facebook either.

Our family discussion about the minimum age for Facebook continued into the evening with my fifteen-, seventeen- and twenty-five-year-olds adding their opinions. It became the "question of the night," with each of their friends who came through our door being subject to interrogation. There seemed to be as many opinions as there were kids. But interestingly enough, the consensus seemed to be that twelve to fourteen years old was the appropriate minimum age. When I asked why, the primary reason was that at twelve kids start seeking more independence from their parents and socializing with their friends. I had expected the young people to say that there should be no age restrictions. Instead, I was surprised by their carefully considered opinions.

My children and their friends explained that young children did not possess the judgment or experience to be on Facebook.

"They will just get themselves into trouble."

"They won't know who to friend and who not to."

"They will friend creepy people."

"They need to learn how to make real friends before they have virtual friends."

In an effort to be honest with you throughout this book, I must make a confession: When Summer was pleading her case for underage use of Facebook, I caved in and said yes. She presented a well-thought-out case, complete with visuals listing why I should allow her to bend the rules. (Okay, maybe I let the Nana and Papa plea get to me.)

Please don't get me wrong, I do not advocate the use of Facebook for an eleven-year-old. With my daughter, we set up a special arrangement. Below are guidelines that we created. You may want to consider similar guidelines if you are inclined to allow your young children with exceptional debating skills to have an account as well.

1. I have complete access to her account, including her password.
2. I can check the activity on her account at any time.
3. For the first few months, she couldn't be online without me.
4. Her privacy settings have to be set to "Only Friends"
5. She can post no personal information on her Profile.
6. She can only friend family members, unless she gets my okay.
7. She cannot use any Applications without my approval.

The use of Facebook by underage kids seems common. I'm not encouraging this, just reporting reality. I would rather have an underage child join Facebook with parental supervision and learn how to use it safely, such as Summer did, instead of joining Facebook without their parents knowing, as McCall did.

The appropriate age to have a Facebook account will vary from child to child, depending on their maturity and judgment. The minimum age according to the Facebook Terms of Service is thirteen[1]. Below is an excerpt from Facebook's Privacy Policy page dated November 19, 2009:

> *If you are under age 13, please do not attempt to register for Facebook or provide any personal information about yourself to us. If we learn that we have collected personal information from a child under age 13, we will delete that information as quickly as possible. If you believe that we might have any information from a child under age 13, please contact us through this help page.*
>
> *We strongly recommend that minors 13 years of age or older ask their parents for permission before sending any information about themselves to anyone over the Internet and we encourage parents to teach their children about safe Internet use practices.*

I support Facebook's policy. Yet I also feel that not all thirteen-year-olds have a "right" to a Facebook account, in the same way that not all teens should be able to drive at age 16. In traveling down the social networking road, your child will need to recognize and avoid many potholes; she will need to navigate some tricky turns. Ideally, you can guide her.

Because young teens are eager to be on Facebook, they are also quite willing to accepting guidelines you create. For example, in my own household, we've agreed that minor kids cannot friend anyone that I do not know. That's part of our family "friending policy."

I believe families benefit when parents work directly with a teen getting started with Facebook. Yes, your child may know more about Facebook than you do. But that doesn't matter. In this case, wisdom from a parent is paramount. Supervise, guide, direct, and teach, just as you will do later when she is learning to drive. Setting up a Facebook account with a young teen is a great way to strengthen your relationship and build some common bonds. Seize the moment!

1 "Statement of Rights and Responsibilities" Section 4 Part 3, Facebook, http://www.facebook.com/terms.php?ref=pf (accessed January 31, 2010).

Is my teen's use of Facebook normal?

Name:	**Linda Fogg Phillips**
Websites:	**www.FacebookForParents.org**

Most parents who take our "Facebook for Parents" classes and workshops want to know if their teenagers are normal.

What is the criteria for "normal" in a teenager? I've given birth to eight children, raised three to finish their teenage years, and still have five more teens to go. I have yet to determine what "normal" is for a teenager. I certainly wish they came with an owner's manual!

By the time I complete my "teenage raising" stage of motherhood, I estimate that I will have survived 54 years of teenage life under my roof. I've concluded that teenagers are exceptional, unreproducible, dynamic individuals who are desperately trying to discover their own identity. A process of discovery is never easy. Teens often struggle. With all this drama, no wonder parents of teenagers worry and ask, "Is this normal?"

On to the question at hand: Yes, it is normal for your teenager to want to build relationships and interact with their friends.

Remember your own teen years? Your friends were more

important than family to you—except, in your day, you were either constantly on the phone or at the local hangout. Now the "local hangout" is Facebook, and this hangout is open 24/7. Have you ever turned off or restricted your child's use of his mobile phone? It is like turning off her oxygen! Facebook is as vital to many teens as their mobile phone. It is how they stay connected socially.

As a concerned parent, is it normal to worry about your children's involvement with Facebook? Sure, that's normal.

When my kids started using MySpace and then Facebook, I was terrified. I had no idea what "social networking" was all about. I was drawn to the horror stories about social networking just as much as my children were drawn to social networking itself. Every time the doorbell rang, I worried that a predator was on my doorstep to lure away one of my beautiful daughters as a result of her involvement on a social networking site!

Solution? I put my foot down: There will be no MySpace or Facebook allowed in our home. End of discussion.

This approach didn't work. My kids still found ways to be part of MySpace and Facebook. Parents in our classes had similar outcomes. Kids know how to acquire a secret account through a second email address, thus avoiding the watchful eye of their parents. The dictatorial style of parenting seems ineffective when it comes to Facebook; it only results in damaged relationships.

"Fine then!" say some parents. "I'll join Facebook, hover over my child's virtual shoulder, and scold them every time they post something that I think is inappropriate!"

That approach won't work either. Your kids can set their privacy settings so that Mom and Dad never see postings they don't want us to see.

If you forbid Facebook or make your presence unwelcome, many teens will find avenues to join Facebook in such a way that you are not present to teach and guide them, and you will forfeit a great opportunity to build a stronger connection between you and your child. By allowing your child Facebook access, you hang onto these powerful options.

Once my children helped me come to my senses and realize how unreasonable I was being, I let them use Facebook. I resolved that I would turn over every rock and peer in every corner of social networking until I uncovered every threat. Some parents ask me if they are being too obsessive in their efforts to protect their children on the Internet. I don't think that is possible. I have devoted myself to learning everything I can about Facebook in an effort to protect our children. This topic matters today, and it will become even more important in the coming years as Facebook continues to grow and become part of our culture.

The flip side of this question is—and yes, parents ask us this question—"Is it normal if my teen is not on Facebook?"

Yes, your teen is still normal. By not having a Facebook account, your teen will not automatically become a social reject. If Facebook is something that does not interest her, then don't worry about it and consider yourself lucky—one less thing to worry about! Some kids simply do not have an interest in "friending" and "unfriending" online, and that is just fine.

Our goal with this book is to answer some important questions so that you can determine if Facebook is a normal part of your teen's life—and your family's life. If so, we want you to be prepared to deal with the potential risks of using Facebook, as well as benefiting from the potential rewards.

Why doesn't Facebook keep everything private?

Name:	BJ Fogg
Websites:	http://bjfogg.com
	http://captology.stanford.edu

One winter evening I logged onto Facebook to see what was new with my friends. I scanned down my Facebook NewsFeed, and I saw that my friend Ben had been tagged in a photo. The image of Ben in my NewsFeed was tiny, just a thumbnail. I couldn't make it out clearly, but I could see some people in the snow. I was curious. What was Ben doing in the snow? I clicked on the thumbnail to see the full-size photo.

Facebook took me to the photo album with Ben's photo, full size. Ah! I could see he was outside of a cabin, all wrapped up, making a snowman. He was with two people I didn't know. And it looked like Ben was having fun.

I was still curious. Where was Ben? Probably in Tahoe. I clicked to see more photos in the album. As I clicked from one photo to the next, I didn't see Ben in any of them. I saw pictures of a baby eating cake in a high chair, and I saw some children opening gifts. I saw lots of people I didn't know. What was going on?

I then realized this photo album on Facebook was not Ben's

album. It belonged to one of Ben's buddies, someone I did not know. His buddy had used Facebook's tagging feature to point out that Ben was in a photo. Since I'm Ben's Friend on Facebook, I received a message about the photo into my News Feed.

Once inside the Facebook Album, I could click around and see all the other photos there, even if Ben was not in the picture. I wasn't the only one who could do this. All of Ben's Friends on Facebook—all 627 of them—could click into the album and see the family vacation at Tahoe.

I wondered if Ben's buddy knew this. Did he really want strangers, such as me, to see the baby eating cake and the children with their presents? Probably not.

Was this a bug in Facebook? I wondered. I did some quick research online, and I found the answer: This was not a bug. This was how Facebook designed their photo sharing system. If one of my Friends is tagged in any of Ben's photos, I can often click through the entire album. Wow. That's sort of creepy, I thought. And I made a note to myself to be careful with my albums and taggings.

When we post content to Facebook, be it photos, videos, or simple status updates, we are hoping to share our lives with our friends. We aren't thinking about sharing with strangers. But often we share with strangers without even realizing it.

What content gets shared on Facebook? The short (incomplete) answer is that all your Friends on Facebook can see anything you post, except for private messages. And likewise, you can usually see anything your Facebook Friends have posted. But this is not a complete answer; it's just a general guideline.

Fully answering this question can be complicated, because frankly, Facebook is a bit complicated. But let me help tune your intuition about Facebook by explaining three "Facebook

Realities." Whenever you have questions about Facebook content sharing, these three facts will help you see the likely answer.

Facebook Reality #1: Facebook is a business, with investors and stockholders.

Facebook Reality #2: Facebook becomes more valuable as a company when you share content widely.

Facebook Reality #3: The Facebook experience is designed for sharing widely.

First of all, Facebook is a business. It's not a charity or a university club. Facebook investors have put millions into Facebook hoping they will eventually get a big return on their money.[1] This means that Facebook has a legal responsibility to make money for those investors. And this leads us to Facebook Reality #2.

As a company, Facebook becomes more valuable whenever people share their content widely. In the Tahoe snowman example above, the fact that I viewed 20 photos on Facebook rather than just the single photo of Ben kept me on Facebook's site longer, viewing more pages, and engaging more with Facebook's features and advertisers. This increased the potential value of Facebook.[2]

And that's where Facebook Reality #3 comes in: The default options on Facebook are set to share your content broadly. For example, today I uploaded a video of me playing blues piano, hitting several wrong notes. Facebook's default setting was to share with "Everyone." I had to take an extra step to share this video only with Friends.

As a parent you may not like Facebook's bias toward sharing widely, but if you think about Facebook as a business, this default makes sense.

I learned about Facebook's bias toward openness in 2007, when I had my first business meeting with Facebook innovators. As the meeting was winding down, I turned to one of the Facebook managers and complained that all my Friends on Facebook could see anything I posted. Sometimes I wanted only my closest friends to see a photo I posted, for example. The response from the Facebook manager: "Yeah, I know," he said. "That's how Facebook works. We believe in sharing openly. That's our philosophy."

"That's not how the world works." I said. "For thousands of years people have been managing relationships differently. We don't share everything with everyone we know."

The Facebook manager's face was unchanged. He repeated the company position: "At Facebook we believe in open sharing. That's our philosophy."

It's been about three years since that meeting, and I've seen how much Facebook has stuck to that philosophy of openness. They haven't made any secret about it.

But they have changed some. The good news here is that Facebook has gradually created more privacy options, empowering you to protect your posts from strangers. But this option is not always the default. To guard your content takes extra work. And many people simply won't take the extra steps.

As Linda and I teach parents about Facebook, we find that once parents understand the business motives behind Facebook's openness bias, they understand Facebook more clearly. The parents then have better intuition about how to use the service and guard their privacy. I hope the same will be true for you.

Now that you have the Facebook Realities and their openness bias in mind, you are ready for the following chapters that explain how privacy works—and doesn't work—on Facebook.

1 http://www.crunchbase.com/company/facebook

2 "Is Facebook Really Worth $10 Billion?" by Gregory Corcoran. May 27, 2009. Wall Street Journal Blog.

Who can see what on Facebook?

Name:	BJ Fogg
Websites:	http://bjfogg.com
	http://captology.stanford.edu

Last week I received a mysterious email at my Stanford account. In his email, a man I'll call "Max" explained that he had created a new invention that would change how the world uses mobile phones. Max wanted to meet with me. He said I was the perfect person to help him turn his idea into a reality.

When I get emails like this, I'm torn. On the one hand, I like to help people. But on the other hand, I have time to meet with only a few people. I have to be selective. In this case, instead of sending a polite reply saying "no," I turned to Facebook to learn more about Max.

It took about 15 seconds to find Max. Thanks to Facebook, I could see Max's profile picture. He didn't look crazy. I could see the names of his Friends, all 262 of them. I could see Max was a fan of Barack Obama and Eddie Izzard. All of this was public information.

The Facebook interface also pointed out that Max and I had two Friends in common. These mutual Friends were people I respected. So I went back to my Stanford email and responded to Max: "Let's start with a short phone meeting."

Max never knew that I looked him up on Facebook.

When you use Facebook, you may assume that only people you accept as Friends can see your profile information and your list of Friends. That's not how it works. At least that's not the default. Let's start with the most troubling issue: What can the world see about you?

The world can see your Big 5

The way Facebook currently works, anyone who knows the email address you used to register for Facebook can see five things about you. Let's call these things the "Big 5":

1. Your Name
2. Your Profile Picture (if you've posted one)
3. Your Current City (if you've listed one)
4. Your Networks (if you've joined one)
5. Pages of which you are a Fan

If you're like most people, the Big 5 list will surprise you because you wouldn't expect such information, especially your picture, to be readily available to most anyone. I agree with you. And you wouldn't expect teens to have their Big 5 exposed, just like adults. But it is. At the time I am writing this chapter, that's how Facebook privacy works.

Personally, I'm not miffed at my Big 5 being on the Internet. I have a website where I share that info anyway. (Your teen does not, of course.) I'm crankier about Facebook revealing my Fan Pages (item #5). Why should the world be able to see that I'm a Fan of Billy Joel? Or any of my fourteen other Fan Pages?

Some might argue that the Big 5 should really be the Big 7,

because by default two additional items appear on your public Facebook listing: your gender and your Friend List. I don't count these two because you can remove these items from your public listing if you follow the steps in Question 13. In contrast, the Big 5 cannot be hidden from public view.

If you don't want the world to see your profile picture, your current city, or your networks, you must not post these items on Facebook. If you've posted this info already, there is no option for hiding it from strangers. But you can delete it. That's not an ideal solution, yet that's how Facebook works these days. And neither you nor I can change that fact.

Limited protection for minors

There's a faint silver lining for kids under 18. Facebook has taken some steps to guard young people against sharing too much. For minors, the "Everyone" setting means at most Friends, Friends of Friends, and Networks—not the entire world. For example, your teen daughter's "Interests" and "Favorite Music" cannot be seen by everyone on Facebook, even if she selects "Everyone" as the option.

Even though Facebook has taken a small step to guard minors, this doesn't always work. Consider one 12-year-old I know. He started a Facebook account and fibbed about his age, knowing that kids under 13 cannot join. When registering, he claimed to be 22. Linda's daughter did something similar. As I see it, you can't blame Facebook for this problem.

However, I believe Facebook could take more steps to protect minors. Here are some nagging issues: If your teen daughter comments on a Friend's Status Update, her comment is available to anyone who can view the original Status Update. If your daughter posts a photo and tags a buddy from school, anyone who is Friends with her buddy can view your daughter's photo and her entire

Album, unless she changes the default setting. Furthermore, when it comes to Search Privacy and teens, "Everyone" does indeed mean the entire world. Teens are given no special protection with the Big 5. That's not good news.

By the time you read this chapter, the last few paragraphs I've written may be outdated. I hope so. Facebook staffers are smart enough to find a better way to balance company goals with personal privacy. I hope they make some changes, especially for minors.

You can control what you share

If you can get over the shock of the Big 5, you'll see the rest of this chapter explains how to control your Facebook content. In general, excepting the Big 5, you determine who sees everything you post on Facebook. In fact, with the new privacy settings, you can now share a photo, a status update, or most other content with only one person, if you choose.

For example, last year I created a video for my sister Linda, wishing her a happy birthday. I didn't want anyone to see it but Linda. So I uploaded the video and used the Facebook sharing options so only she could watch me wishing her happy birthday.

In this case, I used Facebook to share with just one person. However, I could have done the opposite. I could have posted a video and allowed everyone to see it except one person. Perhaps I could have made a video about Linda and let everyone see it except her.

As a parent, you can probably see that this is a two-edged sword. On one side, the new Facebook sharing options allow you and your family to share very precisely, excluding casual friends from viewing your family vacation photos, for example.

But the sword cuts the other way. With the new sharing controls, your child could post a photo and let everyone see it on Facebook except you. Even if you're a Friend of your child on

Facebook, you won't be able to see the photo if she takes the right steps (or the wrong steps, perhaps, from your perspective).

This sharing feature is called Custom Privacy. The interface has an element labeled "Hide this from" and a box where the user enters the name of the person who can't see that content. You probably hope that your child never types your name into that box. But at some point, she probably will, and you won't have any way of knowing.

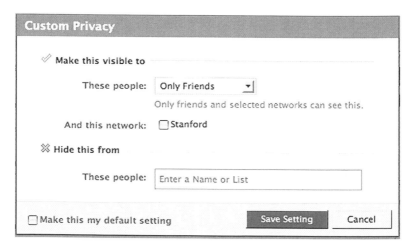

How should a parent deal with this? To get you the best response, I'll have to call on the experienced mom: my sister, Linda. If you haven't done so already, go to Question 6 and read Linda's answer to "Can I See Who My Kids Are Interacting with On Facebook?" Hint: The answer is not a technical trick so much as parental wisdom applied to the dynamics of Facebook.

A general guide on sharing

To help make it clear on how content is shared on Facebook, I've put together a table. I haven't listed all of Facebook's elements (for example, Events are not here), but I've included the most common features. If you're new to Facebook, you may want to copy this page and post it by your computer as a reference while you use Facebook. Eventually, you'll get a sense for what material gets shared and how you can make content more private, if you want.

Who can see what on Facebook?

Everyone can see your Big 5
1. Name
2. Picture Profile (if you've posted one)
3. Current City (if you've listed one)
4. Your Networks (if you've joined one)
5. Pages for which you are a Fan

Everyone can see by default (but you can change the settings)
- Photos you post
- Videos you post
- Any info you post on your Profile Page—activities, interests, etc.

Your friends can always see that you . . .
- Commented on something
- Friended someone new
- Posted on someone's Wall (if they are a mutual Friend)
- Joined a Group
- Became a Fan

Your Friends can see by default (but you can change the settings)
- Your entire list of Friends
- Posts on your own Wall
- Updates to your Status

Caution: The info in the table is likely to change. So please see our website for the latest: www.FacebookforParents.org/sharing

Few things are always private on Facebook

You may be surprised to learn that only a few things are private by default on Facebook. This includes Private Messaging (it's like email) and Chat (it's like instant messaging). And, of course, your password is private. This may not be a complete list, but I'm hard pressed to find other examples.

That said, you should know that nothing guarantees that what you post privately on Facebook will stay private forever. This issue is not unique to Facebook. Any email you write, any text message you send on your mobile phone, any product you buy online—all of these may surface as public information in the future. That's not just our view, but thinkers who have made privacy their obsession have warned of this possibility.[1] No one knows what will happen to digital information in the future.

You should understand that digital information, once uploaded onto the web and copied by a third party, remains forever. Many of our children will be embarrassed some day when their own kids find photos of them at age fourteen striking a provocative pose—or doing something worse.

Balancing benefits and risks

Even though sharing information on Facebook has risks, the rewards outweigh the potential problems, at least for me. I take some baseline precautions. My policy is to never post anything on Facebook that would ruin my career or my personal life. I have the same policy for email. If I have sensitive information, I share it in person, if possible. We've all heard stories of emails going to the wrong people, or being sent to an entire list of people, or being subpoenaed for email records. The same could happen with Facebook.

The challenge here is to help your family understand how to balance the risks and rewards of using Facebook. This service can make our lives better and more fun. Facebook brings people together. But, as with any form of digital communication, you risk sharing information with people you didn't want to. The more you learn about Facebook's sharing controls and privacy settings, the more comfortable you'll be using Facebook and allowing your child to use Facebook.

Just what should you do to guard your privacy? Well, that's the focus of our next chapter. See you there!

1 For example, the Electronic Privacy Information Center maintains a webpage at http://epic.org/privacy/facebook/ with information on Facebook privacy issues.

"How Sticky Is Membership on Facebook? Just Try Breaking Free," by Maria Aspan. New York Times, February 11, 2008, Technology section, http://www.nytimes.com/2008/02/11/technology/11facebook.html?_r=1,

How can I protect my child's privacy? Phase 1: Spring Cleaning

Name:	**Linda Fogg Phillips**
Websites:	**www.FacebookForParents.org**

"Hey McCall." I said to my teenage daughter. "Do you want to help me with a Facebook experiment?"

McCall was always game for adventure, and her wit often surpassed mine. So I wanted my daughter on my team.

"Let's make a Facebook account for Duchess." I said.

"But mom, Duchess is a dog!" McCall reasoned. "She doesn't even have an email address."

"We can fix that," I said. "Besides, I want to see how many people would friend someone they don't even know."

I hurried McCall to my computer. Together we set up an account for "Duchess Pugmire." We completed her Profile Page, positioning her as a teenager in a local private high school. We did not put up a photo of her. Instead, as part of our experiment, we left the generic Facebook "shadow" photo as her profile picture.

(For the record, creating a Facebook account for your dog, cat or pet pig is not allowed. I knew this when I created Duchess' account, but for the sake of research, I hope Facebook will forgive me for this little infraction.)

I pushed the computer keyboard over to McCall and said, "Alright, go ahead and friend as many people as you can. You have 20 minutes. Invite friends of friends, strangers—whatever. Just don't let anyone know that Duchess is connected to you or me."

After 20 minutes I said, "Okay, your time is up. Let's wait and see what happens."

Four hours later we checked Duchess' account. To my surprise, our beloved dog had 59 confirmed Friends on Facebook. The next morning we checked again. Not only she was up to 86 confirmed Friends, but she had 17 pending Friend Requests of her own!

A few prudent people responded to Duchess with messages such as "Do I know you?"

But the usual response was: Confirm, confirm, confirm. And with this, I had access to information about all of Duchess's new Friends, kids and adults alike. Usually, I could also read about their Friends on Facebook. This probably added up to thousands of people. And it was so easy.

A few days later, I was preparing to share the story of Duchess in our "Facebook for Parents" class. At that point, Duchess had 136 Friends on Facebook. Our little experiment showed how

Duchess Pugmire

Wall   Info   Photos   Relatives

Write something...

Attach: 🖼 😊 🎬 📎 ▾   Share

🔍 Filters

Linda Fogg Phillips Your puppies are darling!
about a minute ago · Comment · Like · See Wall-to-Wall

RECENT ACTIVITY

Duchess and Greta Schwalb are now friends. · Comment · Like
Duchess and Linda Sue Purkey are now friends. · Comment · Like
Duchess and David Sneed are now friends. · Comment · Like

View Photos of Duchess (24)
Suggest Friends for Duchess
Send Duchess a Message

some people failed to scrutinize Friend Requests.

I thanked my daughter for her help in this experiment. But then I added:

"Wow, McCall," I said. "Duchess now has more Facebook Friends than you! What do you think about that?"

With a smug look on her face, McCall responded, "Well, I just think that Duchess doesn't have good judgment."

Name:	BJ Fogg
Websites:	http://bjfogg.com
	http://captology.stanford.edu

What are my first steps in securing privacy?

I always find Linda's story about Duchess funny—and accurate. Some people view friending on Facebook as a competition: Whoever has the most Friends wins. Of course, that's not a good game to play when privacy is your concern.

As Linda and I expanded our work with parents on Facebook, we saw the need to create a step-by-step process for protecting family privacy. In response, we created what we call the Three-Phase Facebook Privacy Review. This process applies to you as a Facebook user, as well as your child. Read on to see what we suggest. You may be surprised that the first phase is not to tweak the Privacy Settings. That's Phase 2.

Here's an overview of our three phases. We've created a chapter for each one.

- **Phase 1:** Spring Cleaning (Question 12—this chapter)
- **Phase 2:** Privacy Settings (Question 13)
- **Phase 3:** Daily Routine (Question 14)

You could do the phases in any order, but we think it best to do them in the order we suggest. Our rationale: What's the point of allowing "Only Friends" to see your birthday if some of your Friends on Facebook are actually strangers?

This chapter focuses on what we'll call "Spring Cleaning." This means tidying up your list of Friends and the info you have on your Profile. We offer you two steps in Spring Cleaning.

Step 1: Create a Friending Policy—and stick to it

The most important privacy step you can make on Facebook is to friend wisely. If you friend strangers, for example, you'll be sharing a lot of info with people you don't know—including Friends of their Friends. So you need to start with this step. Figure out who is appropriate to friend. And if you find that you (or your child) is already connected to people you don't want to share your life, you can unfriend them, removing them from your Facebook world. (Don't worry: People are not notified when you unfriend.)

Most kids, I would guess, are like people who friended Linda's dog Duchess. They want to accumulate more Friends. But this is not the best approach to Facebook.

If someone requests to be your Friend on Facebook, and you don't want to be their Friend, you can click "Ignore." Or you can do what I do: Simply leave the request pending. As of right now, I have 793 pending requests. Almost all of these requests are from people I don't recognize.

Requests   Ignore All

🖳 793 friend requests

We suggest you create what we call a "Friending Policy." This is a set of rules you follow in deciding who to friend on Facebook. In our classes with parents, we challenge each person to create a

Friending Policy for their family, to discuss it and agree together who they will and will not friend on Facebook.

You probably have other family policies—who can sleep overnight, who has a key to your house, and so on. In this new world of Facebook, you now need a Friending Policy.

In my own case, I never friend strangers, no matter how often they ask me or how flattering the reason. Because I do research people find interesting, I get emails from strangers asking to be my Facebook Friend so they can stay current with my work. Yes, I'm flattered, but for me, that doesn't persuade. Facebook is for people I know in real life.

What should be your Friending Policy? We can't dictate that for you, just like we can't say who should have a key to your home. But here is a list of questions to bring to the family discussion.

- Can your teen friend strangers?
- Can your teen friend people they've met only online?
- Can your teen friend adults you don't know?
- Is it okay for you to friend your child's Friends?

In most cases, your child will already have dozens, perhaps hundreds, of Friends on Facebook. And at least some of those Friends are, in reality, strangers.

You can see your child's current Friends on Facebook in two ways. The easiest method is to join Facebook and become your child's Friend. This way, you can view all the other Friends your child has. What you see may surprise you. Linda maintains a strict policy that if her children are going to use Facebook, they must friend her. That's the "Linda Rule."

The second way to see your child's Friends isn't as graceful. As a parent, you tell your child you want to see their Friends on Facebook. The child would need to log in and show you. This may or may not work, depending on your approach and your relationship.

Linda and I agree that parents should know who their minor

children friend on Facebook, in the same way you should know who your kids are hanging out with in real life. We realize that some parents take a different approach, but we recommend that all parents with minors on Facebook uphold the Linda Rule.

Step 2: Tidy up your Profile Page

The next step in Spring Cleaning is to go to your Profile Page and look over what's already there. You do this by logging into Facebook and clicking the "Info" tab. Now you can review and edit your information, from Relationship Status to Contact Information.

At this tab you'll see four categories of information:

- Basic Information
- Personal Information
- Contact Information
- Education and Work

As you look over each option and each piece of info, ask yourself: "Am I comfortable sharing this with every single person who is my Friend on Facebook?" If your answer is no, then you should either remove some Friends or remove that piece of information. Often, scaling back the information is the better choice.

As an example, let's look at my info on Facebook. In my own case, I am okay with all of my Facebook Friends having my mobile phone number. So I put it on my Profile Page. But I don't list any political views because I don't see the point of broadcasting a political label. So I leave this option empty.

	Don't show my birthday in my profile. ▾
Current City:	Stanford, CA
Hometown:	
Home Neighborhood:	
Family Members:	Select Relation: ▾
	Add another family member
Relationship Status:	▾
Interested in:	☐ Men ☐ Women
Looking for:	☐ Friendship ☐ Dating ☐ A Relationship ☐ Networking
Political Views:	
Religious Views:	
	Save Changes Cancel

Facebook's interface asks you to list "Family Members." I don't see this serving any useful purpose, so I leave this blank. In fact, I think mapping out your family on Facebook is a risk. At one point, when my own Mom was starting to use Facebook, she put in her maiden name, thinking this would help old friends find her. This is true. But this also created a problem. Because my mom had linked to me as her son, the info about her maiden name was now available to many people. I phoned her to explain that banks use this info to verify my identity. My mom understood this immediately and removed her maiden name from Facebook.

The bottom line on Profile Pages is this: Provide only the information you want all your Facebook Friends to know. You don't have to include everything the Facebook interface requests. In fact, over time, I find myself removing more and more from the Info portion of my Profile Page. I list a few hobbies, my contact info, and my web sites. That's about all. And no one has ever complained.

Here's another way to look at it. On Facebook I don't enter my hometown, my political views, and other such info on my Profile Page because my real-life friends already know this stuff about me. If some Friends on Facebook aren't close personal friends in real life, they don't need to know so much about me. When we become better friends, I'll share more—in person, most likely.

I believe most kids have not taken this safe approach to Facebook. Linda and I have seen teenagers share a lot of personal info on Profile Pages, often way too much. Your challenge as a parent is to negotiate, bribe, plead, and do whatever you can to influence your child to tighten down her Profile Page.

The Facebook interface has changed three times in the year before we wrote this book. And it will continue to change. This makes a printed book a challenging way to share detailed "how to" steps. So after you read the general guidelines in the chapters that follow, we encourage you to watch our helpful videos online about how to protect your family's privacy on Facebook. We will update the videos when Facebook changes some aspect of their Privacy Settings. In a short time with these videos, you will know a lot more about Facebook Privacy Settings than your child. Then you can talk about Facebook privacy with confidence—plus you'll get to see what we look like!

In the two chapters that follow, Linda and I explain the Privacy Settings and then we outline what parents can do routinely—in five minutes each day—to keep kids safe on Facebook.

Resources for parents
See our privacy updates and videos: www.FacebookForParents.org/privacy

How can I protect my child's privacy? Phase 2: Settings

Name:	**BJ Fogg**
Websites:	**http://bjfogg.com**
	http://captology.stanford.edu

When my niece came to visit me for the weekend, I just told her the truth: "I don't think it's a good idea to post your Relationship Status on Facebook. It just causes problems."

My niece and I were Friends on Facebook, and I kept up with her online. Now that we planned a few days together, I wanted to keep it real. It was a good time for heart-to-heart chats.

Her response surprised me. "I know," she said. "But I felt pressured into it by my boyfriend. He wanted everyone to know we were together."

I wasn't happy to hear that her boyfriend controlled this decision. Her Profile stated she was "in a relationship," one of seven options Facebook offers people who want to share this type of info.

"But I'm going to break up with him," my niece said. "Then I'll change my Facebook setting to 'single.'"

"Are you sure?" I said. "How about removing Relationship Status from your Facebook Profile? Just leave it blank. You know how much drama happens because of that relationship setting."

"Oh, I know," she said. "The last time I broke up with my boyfriend, my Friends on Facebook saw that I was suddenly 'single,' and I got all sorts of questions. Total drama."

"But I'm saying you can avoid all that by selecting nothing—just leave it blank. Let me show you how it works . . . "

And with that, my niece and I sat down together and started to review her privacy settings. We selected the blank option for her "Relationship Status" on her Profile Page.

But I didn't stop there. "Let's look over your other settings, okay?"

Together we went through her Profile info and the many privacy settings Facebook offers. There are a lot of them. Even my niece, who was an experienced Facebook user, was surprised by all the options.

For my part, I was troubled by how much my niece was sharing with the world. But one by one, we cranked down the privacy settings on Facebook. Anything that was being shared with "Everyone" or "Friends of Friends" got re-set to be shared only with "Friends" or no one at all.

I thought about the millions of kids who have the wrong privacy settings on Facebook but don't have an adult to help them understand why privacy matters, or what to do about it.

I wish every parent could have this experience with his or her child on Facebook. What Linda and I share in this book should give you confidence to talk with your child about privacy settings. In the ideal world, you and your child will sit down at the computer and review her settings together. And you'll repeat this once a month. The first few times, the review process will take about 30 minutes, but as you become acquainted with the settings, this will go much faster. And after a while, you may become your neighborhood guru on privacy settings. If nothing else, you will feel less anxious about your child using Facebook.

The place to start with securing your privacy was explained in the previous chapter. We call this first phase "Spring Cleaning." To review, the first step in this process is to tidy up your Friend list on Facebook, unfriending anyone who doesn't match your Friending Policy. The next step in Spring Cleaning is to remove any information on your Profile that makes you uneasy.

With your Friend list and Profile info cleaned up, you are now ready to change your privacy settings. There are three overall steps you should take:

Step 1: Review & Adjust Privacy Settings
Step 2: Review & Adjust Application Settings
Step 3: Mark Your Calendar to Repeat Steps 1 and 2

Step 1: Review & adjust privacy settings, one by one

Facebook makes it easy to start reviewing your Privacy Settings. Whenever you are logged into Facebook, you'll see the word "Account" in the upper right-hand corner of the screen. Click on "Account" to see a menu that includes "Privacy Settings." This is how you begin Step 1.

When you select the option for "Privacy Settings," you'll soon see a new screen that lists five categories.

- Profile Information
- Contact Information
- Applications and Websites
- Search
- Block List

To fully set your privacy, you need to click on the first category "Profile Information" and make your selections there. When you are finished, you should come back to this list of five and click on the second category, "Contact Information," and so on. Keep working down the list until you've set your privacy in all five areas.

On the next page is a screen shot of my privacy settings for

Privacy Settings

 Profile Information
Control who can see your profile and who can post to your Wall

 Contact Information
Control who can contact you on Facebook and see your contact information and email

 Applications and Websites
Control what information is available to Facebook-enhanced applications and websites

 Search
Control who can see your search result on Facebook and in search engines

 Block List
Control who can interact with you on Facebook

the first of the five categories, the one about Personal Information. I'm making 12 decisions here. Note that I never let "Everyone" see my info. And sometimes I don't even show info to Friends; I've selected "Only Me."

Because there are so many settings, sometimes people review only the first category of "Profile Information" and forget to do the other four areas. Again, you need to adjust settings for all five categories. At the time I wrote this chapter, you had 44 decisions to make about privacy in Step 1 alone. But don't worry: Once you get the hang of it, you can make these decisions quickly.

Privacy Settings ▸ Profile Information

◄ Back to Privacy	Preview My Profile...
About me About Me refers to the About Me description in your profile	🔒 Only Friends ▾
Personal Info Interests, Activities, Favorites	🔒 Only Friends ▾
Birthday Birth date and Year	🔒 Only Me ▾
Religious and Political Views	🔒 Only Me ▾
Family and Relationship Family Members, Relationship Status, Interested In, and Looking For	🔒 Only Me ▾
Education and Work Schools, Colleges and Workplaces	🔒 Only Friends ▾
Photos and Videos of Me Photos and Videos you've been tagged in	🔒 Only Me ▾
Photo Albums	Edit Settings
Posts by Me Default setting for Status Updates, Links, Notes, Photos, and Videos you post	🔒 Only Friends ▾
Allow friends to post on my Wall	☑ Friends can post on my Wall
Posts by Friends Control who can see posts by your friends on your profile	🔒 Only Friends ▾
Comments on Posts Control who can comment on posts you create	🔒 Only Friends ▾

For most of the 44 decisions about privacy in this category, you'll see a drop-down menu with five options.

- Everyone
- Friends and Networks
- Friends of Friends
- Only Friends
- Customize

There's no way to set an overall privacy level. Instead, for each type of content on Facebook, you must select your level of privacy, one by one. The content ranges from your Personal Info to your Wall to the Posts you make.

If you want to keep your information secure from strangers, you should never select the first three options. Specifically, don't ever select "Everyone," "Friends and Networks," or "Friends of Friends." You can probably guess that selecting "Everyone" is opening your content to the world. But we feel that selecting "Friends and Networks" and "Friends of Friends" is pretty much the same thing.

As you make privacy decisions, we urge you to select "Only Friends" or "Customize." At times, you may want to select "Only Me," which is the most restrictive setting of all. For example, "Only Me" is the option I chose for the "Political and Religious Views" and other information I don't care to share with anyone, not even Friends on Facebook. Yes, I could remove this content, but I find it easier to just opt for "Only Me."

You'll find the "Only Me" option by selecting "Customize" in the drop-down window.

The "Customize" option is a two-edged sword, as I explained in an earlier chapter. Customizing is good for parents because you can tailor who can see a piece of info. But it may be bad for parents because your kids may choose to hide info from you.

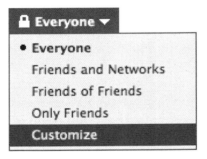

We don't have any scientific evidence for this, but we think most kids are getting better at using these privacy settings (that's a good thing!). The drawback is that as they learn to protect their information from strangers, they also learn to hide information from parents. Teens are likely to not want to share everything they are doing on Facebook with you. (Is that a bad thing? At least they've learned some privacy settings.)

Step 1 is a biggie, because it requires you to walk through five categories and make 44 decisions about privacy. Navigating the interface may be a bit tricky. If you need help, perhaps ask your child to coach you on how to use the interface.

Custom Privacy

    Make this visible to

       These people: `Only Me` ▾

                       Only selected networks and I can see this.

   And this network: ☐ Stanford

    Hide this from

       These people: `Enter a Name or List`

                                  Save Setting   Cancel

In fact, if your child is willing to look at the third area with you—Applications and Websites—you're golden. This could be the start of an important conversation. What you'll both see is 15 items your Friends can share about you with companies who have created applications (or "apps") for Facebook. These are companies outside of Facebook, and sometimes they are not real companies at all. Your Friends can share info about you with many companies unless you say no. Yeah, that's probably a shocker for parents. But that's why we're writing this book: to get you the facts.

Here's how Facebook describes it:

When your friend visits a Facebook-enhanced application or website, they may want to share certain information to make the experience more social. For example, a greeting card application may use your birthday information to prompt your friend to send a card.

If your friend uses an application that you do not use, you can control what types of information the application can access. Please note that applications will always be able to access your publicly available information (Name, Profile Picture, Gender, Current City, Networks, Friend List, and Pages) and information that is visible to Everyone.

Below is a snapshot of what I've done with my own settings. Yes, I've unchecked everything. That means my Friends on Facebook can't share any of this info with companies who have created apps. These decisions make my life on Facebook less exciting because I'm not being invited to apps that people love, but that's okay with me. However, this probably won't be okay with many kids.

In the above paragraphs I've explained the overall approach to setting your privacy on Facebook. I don't explain every single option. To get help on details and to stay current with the latest changes, go to our website for videos we've created just for parents. In these short clips, Linda and I will walk you through each step. It'll be sort of like sitting in our class, except you can wear your bathrobe and slippers.

- ☐ Personal info (activities, interests, etc.)
- ☐ Status updates
- ☐ Online presence
- ☐ Website
- ☐ Family and relationship
- ☐ Education and work
- ☐ My videos
- ☐ My links
- ☐ My notes
- ☐ My photos
- ☐ Photos and videos of me
- ☐ About me
- ☐ My birthday
- ☐ My hometown
- ☐ My religious and political views

Save Changes

See our videos: www.FacebookForParents.org/privacy

Step 2: Review & adjust application settings

If you've made it to Step 2, congratulations! You've done most of the hard work. But don't stop yet. Step 2 is important because, for the most part, you're deciding how companies outside of

Facebook access info about you or your child. Let me explain.

You can divide Facebook into two parts. The first part I call "Basic Facebook." This includes what Facebook, the company, has created for you to use: the Wall, Status Updates, Private Messages, and more. Most of what I use every day is Basic Facebook.

The other part is what I call "Extended Facebook." This includes applications built for Facebook by third parties. When I taught my first Facebook class, my students were building apps. All this would become part of Extended Facebook. In today's world, all the games people play on Facebook are part of Extended Facebook, not Basic Facebook. So if your child is playing FarmVille, she is using an app created by a company named Zynga; it was not created by Facebook.

The first time your daughter decides to use FarmVille, or any other app not created by Facebook, she will need to "Allow" the app to access her information. Facebook requires outside companies to follow a procedure. Right below the "Allow" button for an app, you'll see a sentence like this: "By using FarmVille, you agree to the FarmVille Terms of Service."

If your child clicks "Allow," she is entering into a legal agreement with the makers of FarmVille. It's a good idea to read the Terms of Service. But let's be honest: Who really reads those?

🐾 Allow Access?

Allowing FarmVille access will let it pull your profile information, photos, your friends' info, and other content that it requires to work.

 FarmVille ★★★★
Howdy Ya'll! Come on down to the Farm today and play with your friends. We got plenty of land for everyone. Come and see what everyone is hootin' and hollerin' about.

[**Allow**] or Leave Application

By using FarmVille, you agree to the FarmVille Terms of Service.

Certainly not a teen wanting to play a game. Almost all of us will just click "Allow" and ignore the legal stuff. That's human nature.

Most teens on Facebook have selected "Allow" for many apps. They usually learn about new apps from Friends on Facebook. But teens can also find apps by browsing the directory Facebook has created. With over 300,000 apps offered by outside companies, teens have many choices.

In Step 1 above, you decided what Facebook, Inc., can share about you. Here in Step 2, you're deciding what thousands of companies who create apps can know about you. Again, some of these "companies" are not real companies. They don't have any brand name to protect; they don't have offices, receptionists, or headquarters. Anyone can create these apps for Facebook. And that's why I think you should be on guard.

Under "Application Settings," Facebook allows you to see and change permissions for each app you've started using.

The truth is very few people review Application Settings. And as a result, millions of Facebook users have authorized companies outside of Facebook to access their data.

One of the most admirable apps for Facebook is called "Causes." This app helps you rally people to support a cause and raise money. I've used the Causes app for over two years; it's one of the best apps ever made for Facebook.

Under Application Settings, I can see what permissions I've given to Causes, and I can change those permissions.

In this case, I've allowed Causes to:

- Access my data even when I'm not using the application
- Send me emails
- Publish to streams

I could remove any of those permissions at this step. And for some apps I do just that.

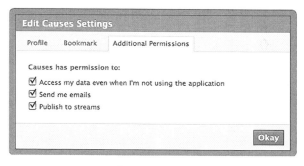

As you can imagine, few teenagers will do Step 2 without some prompting. Millions of teens have given permission to companies to access their data, but they did so without thinking. They just wanted to play FarmVille, or Mafia Wars, or—in the best case—support a good cause using Causes.

The best practice is to inspect every app under "Application Settings." You do this by clicking on "Edit Settings." What permissions have you granted this app? If you are not using an app listed, we suggest you remove it by clicking on the X in the far right. It's good housekeeping.

For example, if I click on the X to remove the app "Causes," this app will no longer have access to my data. (In my own case, I won't remove Causes. I like this app and the people behind it.)

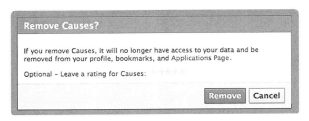

As I write this chapter, I see about a dozen apps on my own list that I'm no longer using. I need to remove them. Time for another round of housekeeping! And that brings us to Step 3.

Step 3: Mark your calendar to repeat steps 1 and 2

The best way to protect privacy on Facebook is to do the steps above—and to repeat those steps regularly. I think once a month is adequate.

Each time I review my privacy settings, I find something I want to change. Sometimes I'm surprised I missed a setting before. For example, I may find I created a new Photo Album last week and forgot to change the default setting of "Everyone" to my usual "Only Friends."

Make privacy a priority

At the start of this chapter I explained how I helped my niece adjust her privacy settings. Notice that I didn't start the conversation by saying her Profile Page revealed too much. I started with something small and relevant to her current worries. When she realized I knew a lot about Facebook privacy—and how much she'd overlooked—she welcomed further help from me. Also, by being Facebook savvy, I also reinforced my standing as a cool, trusted uncle :-).

If your child has come to you, as her parent, for help on setting privacy on Facebook, she deserves a gold medal—and perhaps you do too. I can't imagine this happening very often. The reality is that it's up to you to make privacy a priority for your child and other family members. The fact that you're reading this book is evidence you already know this fact and that you care enough to do something about it.

In this chapter, I've tried to give you the big picture of what you need to do to help protect your child's privacy. I haven't shared all the detailed little steps, every setting and feature. A book can't convey this well. Instead, we have created videos online that will show you the details and keep up with any changes Facebook makes (and yes, they will make changes).

In addition to the steps I've explained in this chapter, you should create a daily routine to help guard your child on Facebook. In the next chapter, Linda explains what you can do quickly and easily each day to help protect your child on Facebook. This routine takes about five minutes, and it's interesting to do. We hope you make this a habit.

Resources for parents
See our privacy updates and videos: www.FacebookForParents.org/privacy

How can I protect my child's privacy? Phase 3: Daily Routine

facebook

Name: **Linda Fogg Phillips**
Websites: **www.FacebookForParents.org**

As our kids run out the door for the day, we ask "Did you brush your teeth? Did you floss?" When our kids get in the car with us, we subconsciously listen for the "click" of their seat belts before we back out of the garage. Once a year, we take them in for health check-ups to ensure that their immunizations are up to date.

Why do we have these "check" systems? As parents, we want to protect our children in all aspects of their lives. We want to protect their teeth from decay, protect them in the car from a possible accident, and protect their bodies from disease. In today's world, we now need to have a system in place, a daily routine, to ensure the safety of our children on Facebook.

On the following page you'll fine the "Child-Protection Routine" we suggest you do each day. Most of the steps assume you are Friends with your child on Facebook.

Step 1: Log onto Facebook daily

We suggest you log onto Facebook each day. It takes only a few minutes to see what's new in your child's Facebook world. You will soon discover a pattern to when your child and her Friends post and make comments. You can time your daily check accordingly. Even though my children jokingly claim that I am "stalking" them by doing this, I see it as no diffferent from when they ask to go to a party. I call the hosting parent to make sure there will be adult supervision. In my view, my underaged children still need adult supervision at the ongoing "Facebook party."

Step 2: Look over your child's Profile Page

Go to your child's Profile Page. There are a few ways to do this. The most obvious is to view your entire list of Friends and click on your child's listing. I find it simpler to browse my News Feed and click on any item that includes one of my kids.

If you have more than one or two children (like I do), you can make it easy to see their Facebook activities at once by setting up a Friend List that contains only your children. You can take this to the next level. If you're Friends with some of your child's Friends, you can also set up a list for them. These lists will filter the content in your News Feed so it only has items relevant to your kids. From the News Feed listings, you can click to the Profile Page of your children.

Once you are on your child's Profile Page, here are some of the important items that you will be able to see:
- Status updates
- Posts of photos and videos
- Photos that your child has been tagged in

- Comments made on her page
- Comments she has made on her Friends' pages
- Applications she has used
- Group or fan pages she has joined

Step 3: Read the items on your child's Wall

The central feature of any Profile Page is the Wall. By looking at your child's Wall, you can see a history of your child's activities on Facebook. As you can imagine, the Wall will give you invaluable insight into your child's life.

In this chapter, I've included a sample screenshot of the Facebook Wall for my dog Duchess. Hmmm. I see she just had five babies. (Hey, Duchess: I'm just making sure you're doing okay.)

Step 4: Look over your child's Friends

On your child's Profile Page, you can usually see a list of her Friends, including people she has recently friended. Most Facebook parents would agree this is as important as knowing who your child's friends are in the real world.

I suggest you check if the number of Friends has changed for your child recently. This will help you talk with your child about who they have friended, and who has friended them. If someone has de-friended your child—or vice versa—there's probably a story there. You may want to ask about it.

By clicking on the name of any Friend of your child, you'll be taken to that person's Profile Page. In this way, you can see information about that person. The information may be limited, but you can always see something. You can learn a lot about your child by keeping informed about their Friends on Facebook.

Step 5: Check your child's Info Page

While on your child's Profile Page, click on the Info tab. You don't need to check this daily, since the information there probably won't change often. But do make it a habit to review what your child has posted. This info is what your child is sharing with Friends—and possibly the world.

In screenshot of Duchess's Info Page, I see she has revealed more about herself than what I would want my children to share. As you look over your child's information, if anything there makes you squirm, it's a good time to coach your child about what is appropriate to share.

Also, as you review your child's Info Page, note if any of the content has changed recently. Has your child added or deleted anything? If she has, try to understand why. There's always a reason.

Step 6: Look at photos of your child & browse entire albums

When your News Feed says your child has been tagged in a photo, go see the photo. Photo sharing is one of the best aspects of Facebook. And for a parent, these photos can be informative. What's not so obvious is that you can—and should—browse through the entire album. The other photos in an album will give you a sense of your child's social circle that you don't ordinarily see.

Call it spying if you want, but a lot of other people are privy

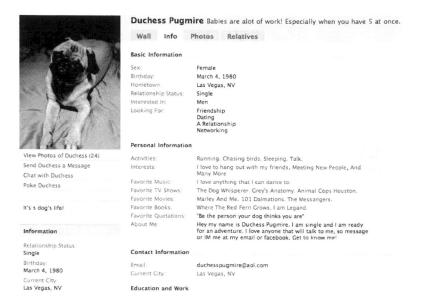

Duchess Pugmire Babies are alot of work! Especially when you have 5 at once.

Wall   Info   Photos   Relatives

Basic Information

Sex:	Female
Birthday:	March 4, 1980
Hometown:	Las Vegas, NV
Relationship Status:	Single
Interested In:	Men
Looking For:	Friendship
	Dating
	A Relationship
	Networking

Personal Information

Activities:	Running. Chasing birds. Sleeping. Talk.
Interests:	I love to hang out with my friends, Meeting New People, And Many More
Favorite Music:	I love anything that I can dance to.
Favorite TV Shows:	The Dog Whisperer. Grey's Anatomy. Animal Cops Houston.
Favorite Movies:	Marley And Me. 101 Dalmations. The Messangers.
Favorite Books:	Where The Red Fern Grows. I am Legand.
Favorite Quotations:	"Be the person your dog thinks you are"
About Me:	Hey my name is Duchess Pugmire. I am single and I am ready for an adventure. I love anyone that will talk to me, so message or IM me at my email or facebook. Get to know me!

Contact Information

Email:	duchesspugmire@aol.com
Current City:	Las Vegas, NV

Education and Work

View Photos of Duchess (24)
Send Duchess a Message
Chat with Duchess
Poke Duchess

It's s dog's life!

Information

Relationship Status
Single
Birthday:
March 4, 1980
Current City:
Las Vegas, NV

to those pictures as well. In reality what you are doing—looking at photos, browsing the album—is typical Facebook behavior. Friends do this all the time with their Facebook Friends. My philosophy is: If others can see what my child has posted on Facebook, then Mom should be able to as well.

Step 7: Talk about Facebook with your child

Find opportunities to work Facebook into your daily conversation with your children. For example, you might say, "Hey, I saw on Facebook that your friend John just got accepted to college. That's great!" Or you can make comments such as, "I really like your updated profile picture."

The point of Step 7 is to make Facebook a normal part of your life and your discussions.

My favorite place to hold Facebook conversations is in the car, while I chauffer my children to school and sports practices. I have them captive! Even a simple question such as "Did you see that funny picture that Jason posted on Facebook this morning?" can open the door to more real-life communication.

Another great place to talk about Facebook is at the dinner table. There's always a new, hot topic on Facebook. For example, you could ask what your child thinks about the girl who started a Facebook Page named "Sign the Petition to get Jenny Ungrounded!" Or you can show your awareness of Facebook with comments such as, "It's amazing how fast Facebook is growing. I read in the paper that Facebook now has 400 million users." When your child knows you are a savvy citizen of the Facebook world, you create a foundation for parenting your child in that world.

Facebook is an invaluable resource

As you take steps each day to protect your child on Facebook, you will come to appreciate how this online service opens a window into your child's life and heart. A clear view of your child's emotions and thoughts may not be evident otherwise. As a busy mom concerned with my family's well-being, I am grateful every day for the insight Facebook gives me into the lives of my children.

What are the privacy loopholes on Facebook?

Name: **BJ Fogg**
Websites: **http://bjfogg.com**
http://captology.stanford.edu

One day last summer, I got a Facebook message saying I'd been tagged in a photo. When I clicked to view the image, I saw a shot of a Halloween party with my college friends. The year was 1987.

The photo captured about 30 of us, all dressed up and posing for the camera. I looked from one face to another, smiling at the outrageous costumes and the good memories. And then I stopped smiling. I had found myself in the photo. I was dressed as Chairman Mao.

"Oh, no!" I thought.

I wasn't making a political statement back then. I had recently returned from Shanghai, and the clothes I'd brought home served as an easy and unusual costume. I never expected that years later my costume choice would be posted on Facebook and live forever.

Logical or not, when I viewed the old photo on Facebook, I felt regret. So I took control. I found my name under the image, and I untagged myself.

This isn't my only story about untagging a photo on Facebook. In the last year, I've probably untagged ten photos, both old and new. My Friends who post these images are well meaning, but despite their good intentions, I review each tagged photo and I consider: Is this image what I want my 816 Friends on Facebook to see? Once in a while, I'm uneasy. So I untag.

My college students tell me it's uncool to untag. But I don't care. In the real world, I don't let people stick ugly signs in my front lawn. For me, my Facebook account is like a front lawn: You are choosing how you present yourself to the world.

When most parents worry about privacy on Facebook, they think about Facebook Inc. selling data to advertisers or shifty strangers plotting harm. Few think about how Friends on Facebook can be a threat to privacy. Even if you choose the most restrictive settings, your Friends can reveal things about you or your family you don't want shared.

In previous chapters we described two of the biggest privacy threats on Facebook.

The Big 5
Info Facebook shares about you, no matter what (see Question 11)

Sharing information with apps
Info you share with companies if you use their apps (see Question 13)

Now I'm going to explain more privacy loopholes, including how Friends can unwittingly leak information about you or your child.

Privacy loopholes in tagging & photo sharing

Sharing photos on Facebook is among the most popular activities. In fact, the early staffers at Facebook added this feature during their first few months as a company. Today, Facebook is the #1 site for photo sharing.

But with photo sharing comes some privacy loopholes. Before we get into the nitty-gritty of the loopholes, you need to understand what "tagging" is on Facebook. (We've explained tagging in another chapter, so if you know this stuff, skip ahead to the next section.)

What's "tagging"?

One of the coolest features on Facebook is also one of the scariest: tagging.

When you "tag" a photo on Facebook, you are identifying people in the photo. Facebook records and shares this information. For example, if I post a photo to Facebook that has my sister Linda in it, I can take a few simple steps to tag her. This identifies her to anyone who hovers their cursor over the photo, and it also connects her name and profile to the photo. (Tagging also works for videos and some other aspects of Facebook, but it is most common with photos.)

Any Friend of the person posting the photo can tag it. If I upload a picture of Linda and I don't tag it, my mom—or any of my other Facebook Friends—can tag it. Teens and adults alike find pleasure in looking at photos and tagging people in them. As a result, almost any photo of you posted on Facebook will eventually be tagged.

Every time you get tagged in a photo, you will get an email message from Facebook with a link so you can see the photo. Your Friends on Facebook might also be notified. This notification without your approval is one reason tagging can get dicey.

People tagging you can reveal too much

Tagging can get personal, because Facebook creates a direct link from my Profile Page to all photos and videos in which I'm tagged. These are not just the photos I've uploaded. The link under my mugshot connects to all photos tagged with my name, no matter who posted the photo.

Unpleasant people can use tagging to hurt or annoy. Consider this example: Let's suppose Laverne is upset with Shirley. Laverne could post an unflattering photo of Shirley on Facebook and tag her. Then all of Shirley's Friends could see it.

Let's look at a less obvious scenario: Suppose that Laverne uploads a photo of a naked woman's back to Facebook. This is not a picture of Shirley, but Laverne tags Shirley in the photo. The tag implies that Shirley is the naked woman. (In this case, when the photo or the tag is inappropriate, Facebook provides a feature for reporting the problem. But until that action happens, people can view the photo. Yeah, it's not ideal.)

Remember that college photo of me dressed as Chairman Mao? Recall how that picture implied something I didn't like. Imagine every photo ever taken of you, some you don't even know about, that could be uploaded onto Facebook. I think it's fair to say tagging can be a privacy loophole.

Two solutions to "tagging" problems

You can't stop people from tagging you, but there are two things you can do to minimize embarrassment. First, when Facebook notifies you by email that you've been tagged, go see the photo! If you don't like it, untag yourself.

The next step is more dramatic. But it's a step I've taken for myself. You can change your privacy settings so only you can see that you've been tagged in a photo. Your Friends don't get notified, and people can't search for photos of you using tags. You'll find this option under Privacy Settings > Profile Information.

A tag can open the entire photo album

As described in the story opening Question 10, when you or a Friend gets tagged in a photo, all your Friends can view any photo in that entire album, unless the album creator takes steps to restrict access. For example, suppose you join me at a restaurant, and you take our photo and upload it to Facebook in an album you call "Friends at Dinner." You tag me in that photo. Any of my Friends on Facebook can see that photo of us, unless you change the default settings on your album. But here's the privacy loophole: In this case, all my Friends on Facebook will be able to see all the photos in your album, even if they are not your Facebook friends.

This seems to happen a lot. A tag will bring you inside an album, and then you can view all the other photos there. You can see who else has been tagged. You can also read comments made by strangers. And strangers can read comments you make on photos in that album.

How to protect your photos against unwanted eyes

One way to protect your photos from unwanted eyes is to create several albums, each private for certain groups. My family photo album is not the same as my photo album for Friends, which is not the same photo album for colleagues.

To share a photo, you must create an album. By default any new album is viewable by the public, as shown in the screenshot that comes next.

Album Name:	Photos from Our Class Field Trip
Location:	
Privacy:	🔒 Who can see this?
	Everyone ▾

This means that you have to take an extra step to restrict everyone in the world from being able to see photos in the new album.

Remember, Facebook's bias is toward making everything you share available to everyone. In recent revisions, the Facebook team has done a better job of showing you how to control who sees what. However, you can see that restricting access to what you share takes one extra step at least. Sometimes we forget to take this step—or we just can't be bothered. But the small extra step outlined above can save you a lot of headaches if your work colleagues see your Chairman Mao outfit.

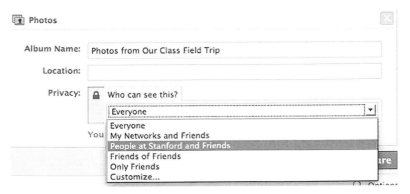

People posting on your wall

Just as well-meaning Friends can tag you in photos you don't like, they can also post things to your Wall you don't like. This happens to me about once a week. Imagine how often teens post unwise messages on each other's Walls.

Let me give you an example. A few months ago, I was in Europe speaking and teaching. When I'm away from home, I try not to broadcast it on Facebook. But my Friends don't follow this guideline. Sometimes they post to my Wall: "Hope you're enjoying Gelato in Italy!" or "Are you staying warm in Norway?" My Friends could have sent me a private Message, but it's easiest for people to post on my Wall. Usually, all your Facebook Friends can see the post. If you haven't set your privacy restrictions, then your Wall is open to the entire world.

If you've spent time on Facebook, you've seen awkward messages posted to the Walls of your Friends: health problems, personal insults, romantic break-ups, and so on.

Luckily, with the Wall you can take control. You can delete anything that gets posted to your Wall, you're instantly notified by email if somebody does post, you can block problem posters, and you can even hide your Wall from everyone. Most people, unfortunately, don't take these steps. They stick with the Facebook default of allowing everything to be shared, even if it is a misguided Wall Post from a Friend who clumsily reveals your secrets.

Networks are full of strangers

Facebook creates what they call "Networks" to segment people by school or workplace. On Facebook, there's a network for people who work at Yahoo, or at HP, or at Starbucks. If you have a work email address from those companies, you can join those networks.

Facebook also has networks for colleges, like Stanford, as well as for high schools. Anyone with a Stanford email address can join the Stanford network.

What's the point of Networks? Good question.

When Facebook was just for college students, Networks grouped the early users by university: Harvard, Yale, Stanford, and so on. And people felt comfortable sharing widely within their Network. But today, with so many Facebook users, Networks serve little purpose in my view, except for being a privacy loophole.

In fact, I recommend you don't join any Networks at all, unless it's a benefit to your professional life.

I'm part of the Stanford Network on Facebook. There are over 50,000 people in that network. I obviously don't know all of them. And I don't want to share my photos, videos, or status updates with all those strangers, even if they are associated with Stanford.

The only real use for Networks is to label yourself as part of a larger organization, be it a company or a school. You don't have to join any networks at all on Facebook. I did. I like being part of the Stanford community, and I think it's good for people to see this on my Profile. I could allow people in the Stanford Network—all 50,563 of them—to see my photos or my Wall. But I don't.

In my view, you and your family should not allow people in Networks to see any of your information on Facebook. It's a loophole.

Stay vigilant, stay updated

Facebook may have other privacy loopholes I did not explain in this chapter. But I believe I've covered the most critical. As the Facebook interface and policies change, you may find that one or more of the loopholes I explain here has been fixed or at least mitigated in some way. If so, good for Facebook!

Facebook can't really re-code your Friends so they stop posting private info on your Wall or posting old college photos that make you squirm. But perhaps in the future, Facebook will allow us to approve tags, filter the posts to our Wall, and so on, giving us more control over what people see about our lives.

As with other aspects of Facebook, you need to keep learning and stay updated. To keep current with the latest on privacy loopholes, you can see our special page, where we offer updates to this chapter, as well as videos that show more than a book's printed page can convey.

Reference

For updates and videos on this topic, see www.FacebookForParents.org/loopholes

How can Facebook apps threaten privacy?

Name:	**BJ Fogg**	
Websites:	**http://bjfogg.com**	
	http://captology.stanford.edu	

Have you heard about "FarmVille"? "We're Related"? "Pillow Fight"?

These are names of applications for Facebook. They allow people to play Facebook games together, send virtual gifts, take fun quizzes, and more. Well over 300,000 such "apps" are available for Facebook users.

Some apps on Facebook are very compelling, even addictive. But the real problem for parents is that these apps can leak information about your child.

Apps are like a mall full of video arcades. Kids can come play, but in order to get into each arcade, they have to hand over their I.D. While they're playing, the arcade provider has access to some of their information.

When your child uses an app, the app vendor can see their name, their birthday, their hometown, and more. The owner of the mall—in this case, Facebook, Inc.—has set out ground rules for the arcade vendors. Vendors are not supposed to store this information longer than 24 hours. But of course some do. Who knows what they might do with this information later?

Facebook works hard to police the app vendors, but there are so many, they can't keep up. The Facebook team responds mostly to complaints, meaning they mostly perform damage control. But as a parent, you don't want your kid's information misused in the first place.

Here are the bits of information Facebook shares with people who create apps. We've created this list from Facebook's own disclosure statement.

Let's suppose you use the "BJ's Pillow Fight" app. Once you start using my Facebook app, I may then have access to these things about you:

- your name
- your profile picture
- your gender
- your birthday
- your hometown location (city/state/country)
- your current location (city/state/country)
- your political view
- your activities
- your interests
- your musical preferences
- television shows in which
- movies in which you are interested
- books in which you are interested
- your favorite quotes
- your relationship status
- your dating interests
- your relationship interests
- your network affiliations
- your education history
- your work history
- your course information
- copies of photos in your photo albums
- metadata associated with your photo albums (e.g., time of upload, album name, comments on your photos, etc.)
- the total number of messages sent and/or received by you
- the total number of unread messages in your in-box
- the total number of "pokes" you have sent and/or received
- the total number of wall posts on your Wall
- a list of user IDs mapped to your friends
- your social timeline
- notifications that you have received from other applications
- events associated with your profile

Anyone can become authorized to create apps for Facebook. No credentials are required. When I taught the first-ever class on Facebook apps at Stanford, all 75 of our students created apps for Facebook. It cost them nothing, and they had access to millions of Facebook users. Our students could access certain types of info about any person who decided to use their apps.

As Facebook describes it in a disclosure statement: "an application . . . can generally access the same information that you can see about yourself and your friends."

Remind your child: When you agree to use an app, you are friending a stranger, and friending everyone they choose to share that information with. Few Facebook users think about apps in this way.

Many parents will find this next fact even more troubling: Even if your child doesn't use any applications on Facebook, her information may still be available to app creators if any of your child's friends uses an app. As Facebook explains: "An application . . . that your friend connects with can access the same information about you that the friend can see."[1]

Wow.

So what can you do?

Facebook offers a privacy setting that blocks app creators from accessing information about you or your child. (I explain this in Question 13.) This is the safest approach. But taking this approach also means you can't often use the full functionality of many apps on Facebook. No "FarmVille" or "We're Related" or "BJ's Pillow Fight" or any other app your kid thinks is fun.

Should you stop your child from using apps on Facebook? I can't make that decision for you, just like I can't say if your child should go to the arcade mall. In my view, Facebook apps create one of the most complicated privacy situations online today.

Facebook's official Platform page describes it this way:

"We do not own or run the applications and websites that you interact with through Facebook Platform, and while we try to enforce standards to protect your information, we cannot guarantee that they will follow our rules. You are responsible for evaluating whether you want to use an application or website and whether you want to share information with it." [2]

But are underaged children capable of evaluating and agreeing to the implicit contract offered by a tempting Facebook application? Linda and I don't think so.

The solution? Set your privacy settings for maximum privacy. As advised by Facebook:

"If you want to change the information that these third parties can access about you when you or a friend uses Facebook Platform, you should modify your privacy settings."

When apps first launched on Facebook in 2007, they were an instant hit. I was part of Facebook's Platform launch event, showing off two apps my own company had created. Since that day in 2007, the Facebook team in charge of apps has made many changes, mostly improvements. I'm quite sure the app landscape on Facebook will continue to grow and change. For the latest update on apps, including specifics about what app creators can learn about your child, see our page here: **www.FacebookforParents. org/apps**

Of course, if you haven't done so already, don't forget to read Question 13 where I talk about the privacy settings related to third-party apps on Facebook.

References

1 http://www.facebook.com/settings/?tab=privacy&section=applications&field=learn

2 http://www.facebook.com/terms.php

How do I protect my child from strangers or unwanted friends?

| Name: | **Linda Fogg Phillips** |
| Websites: | **www.FacebookForParents.org** |

From the moment that our baby is born and placed in our arms, a foremost concern is how to protect our child from the evils of the world. As they learn to walk, we hold their hand. As they learn to ride a bike, we equip them with training wheels and a helmet. Our "mother bear" instinct emerges when our child receives criticism or scrutiny from an unwelcome source. As our children grow and develop, we carefully select playgroups and associations with other children that we deem appropriate friends.

So what happens when our children venture into the social networking world where we as parents have such limited ability to selectively guide our children's choices of friends? Often, we aren't even familiar with the individuals that our children choose to friend on Facebook, and the scariest part of that is that neither are they.

Let's look at the case of Sarah. Sarah is in the eleventh grade at the local high school. With her parents' approval she maintains a Facebook account. She often friends "Friends of Friends." As a result, this has increased her exposure to many other people with whom she has no personal connection. She has also accepted friending requests from random people that found her through other Facebook sources. When it comes to Facebook Friends, our children often mistake quantity for popularity. Sarah's friending policy has been "the more the merrier," as she has tried to see how many Friends she could acquire, as if it were a contest.

One night Sarah received a message from a Facebook Friend she didn't even know or recall friending. Not wanting to be impolite, she replied. This Friend soon began sending her private messages only she could see. Sarah engaged in several exchanges before she got an uncomfortable feeling. The strange Friend wouldn't let up. Sarah was mature enough to tell her parents about it. This Facebook Friend was then blocked.

But Sarah's parents had a hundred questions: What does this Facebook Friend know about you? Does he know where you live? Does he know where you go to school? Is there any way we can report him to the police? Sarah wasn't even sure she could answer any of the questions. To say the least, Sarah and her parents were unnerved. They worried about what could happen next.

Children generally see the Internet as a fairly benign place to interact with people that they do not know. "After all, what could happen?" the child reasons, "I'm not face-to-face with that person, and they don't even know where I live." Or do they?

Danielle Phillips I love when random people text me ♥
January 20 at 10:38pm · Comment · Like

👍 2 people like this.

    Linda Fogg Phillips I don't! Please tell me they aren't strangers. Haven't I taught you not to talk (text) to strangers yet?
    January 21 at 1:03pm · Delete

    Danielle Phillips mom reallyy
    January 21 at 4:26pm

Write a comment...

How to protect your child from strangers on Facebook

The Privacy Settings on Facebook are your first step in protecting your child from strangers. You can sit down with your child and review those settings with her. As you take the steps we outline in Questions 12 and 13, you can reinforce what you have taught your child over the years about selecting good friends. Remember: Your teen may know a lot about Facebook, but they don't have better judgment than you. As with other issues in this book, the key is to merge your judgment with your teen's "know how" of the online world.

Your child should know it's okay to select "ignore" in response to unwanted Friend requests on Facebook. An even better approach may be to neither "accept" or "ignore." Just don't do anything. Why? Because once your child hits the "ignore" button, that individual can yet again request her as a Friend. This can escalate into harassment with repeated Friend requests from the same individual. If your child does nothing, then that individual doesn't have the ability to repeatedly send Friend requests. He is essentially in limbo waiting to be confirmed as a Friend, which will never happen.

Another option for dealing with unwanted Friends on Facebook is to block them. If you block someone, they can see nothing about you on Facebook. They cannot see your profile, your comments, or interact with you in any way. All ties your child currently has with the blocked person will be broken, and that individual will not be able to contact your child through Facebook. (Wouldn't it be nice to be able to do this in the real world?)

So how do you go about blocking someone? You can block a person by listing his or her name in the "Block People" box at the bottom of your Privacy Settings page.

Privacy Settings ▸ Block List

◄ Back to Privacy

Block People

People you have blocked will not be able to interact with you on Facebook. Any Facebook friendships or relationships you currently have with that person will be broken. Note that blocking someone may not prevent all communications and interactions in applications, and does not extend to elsewhere on the Internet.

You have not added anyone to your Block list.

Person		Block
Email		Block

We know that we can't raise our children in a bubble, nor would we want to. We teach our children sound judgment in selecting their friends, whether it be in person or in the virtual world. Your child will not always make the best choices about their Facebook Friends or real-life friends, but we can help them recognize when they've made a bad decision and how to reverse it. Remember, good judgment comes from experience.

How can I prevent bullying on Facebook?

Name:	**Linda Fogg Phillips**
Websites:	**www.FacebookForParents.org**

I have to make another confession. I've delayed writing this chapter because it deals with a terrible subject—bullying on Facebook. I've seen the devastating effects of this practice first-hand. When such behavior occurs among adults, we call it intimidation, coercion, or harassment, each of which is a criminal offense. With minors, we call it bullying, and the results can be far more psychologically damaging.

Bullying that takes place via email, social networking sites, and texting is called cyberbullying. It crosses all platforms and needs to be confronted at every level, not just on Facebook.

Our own children may have been involved in bullying, as the victim, perpetrator, or both. Consider the simple act of posting an unflattering photo on Facebook, or of one sibling verbally insulting another. As I see it, that's bullying.

On the other end of the spectrum is the type of bullying that is so traumatizing that it causes the victim to take her own life. The questions that we need to ask ourselves are: Where does cyberbullying start, how does it escalate, and how do we prevent it?

I have permission to share the experience of a teenage friend of mine who was a victim of bullying. I'll call her "Angie," though that's not her real name.

Angie is a bright young woman who, at the time, attended a prestigious high school. During her sophomore year, she drew some negative attention from a small group of neighborhood kids, both boys and girls. This started with verbal assaults. Then other kids at school joined in the bullying. The assaults began coming in through emails, text messages, and of course MySpace and Facebook. Angie withdrew into her shell as she was being publicly humiliated on the social networking sites. She read such posts as:

"You are so stupid you should be in kindergarten."
"Why don't you go find a hole and climb in it?"
"We are having a party, but no losers allowed."

Many adults and school authorities, once informed, viewed these actions as "typical kid stuff." The abuse continued, and Angie sank deeper into depression. Her parents tried to encouraged her to "shake it off" and to "ignore those kids."

When Angie attempted suicide, everything changed. Her parents pulled her out of school and enrolled her in a program out-of-state to help her recover from depression and trauma.

Nine weeks later, Angie returned home and to school only to be confronted by the same tormentors. This time, they resorted primarily to cyberbullying, using Facebook and Myspace, both places with little adult supervision. Although Angie blocked them as Friends on Facebook and cancelled her MySpace account, the bullies still found ways to post comments such as:

"You are better off dead."
"Go jump off a bridge."
"Why don't you go hang yourself?"

Still fragile, Angie took the last suggestion to heart and planned her second suicide attempt. This time her parents were prepared. They withdrew Angie from school permanently and aggressively pursued the offending bullies.

Unlike similar stories you have heard in the media, this true story has a happy ending. Angie is currently attending college and works as a counselor at summer youth programs.

"I will do everything in my power," she says, "to stop bullying before it ever starts. I don't want another child to go through what I went through."

Angie's mother has become an active crusader against bullying. She's involved with school districts, youth programs, and churches. As I spoke with her, she tearfully explained that her biggest regret is that she did not recognize the bullying sooner and take aggressive action immediately.

The "bullies" in Angie's story came from homes that are middle to upper income. I know many of the families. Their parents are respectable citizens who taught their children good values. The bullies knew better! So what happened?

The parents either did not stop the bullying soon enough, or they didn't realize the harm their children were causing. It's sad that not one of the offending teens resisted the pack mentality that started as "benign teasing" (if there is such a thing). Even Angie and her mother recognize that Angie did things that provoked the bullying to continue and did not address the issue quickly enough.

As Facebook facilitates our ability to communicate with each other, it speeds up the rate at which a few careless comments can escalate into a tornado of abuse. Peer pressure, impulsivity, and the power of gossip can sweep dozens of teens into a public feud in a matter of hours. Sometimes all the abuse is directed at one child. With today's technology, not much separates one insulting post from mass public persecution.

Bullying once took place behind the backstop on the playground, where adults were not supervising. Now the playground has expanded to include the Internet. One difference is that today the bullying is often invisible to parents. We need to make it visible, by joining Facebook and monitoring teen interactions, the same way we keep an eye on the playground.

Abuse that takes place on the Internet can be documented. This evidence opens bullies to possible disciplinary or even criminal action. Thanks to Facebook's policy, Angie's parents have complete documentation of the abuse, which they used in a court to acquire restraining orders. In an effort to preserve the futures of the accused, they stopped short of pressing criminal charges. Not all parents of a bullied child will show such restraint.

Early intervention is the solution. Here's a hopeful example: A high school in Seattle suspended 28 students who joined a Facebook Group to victimize another student. I commend the principal for taking quick action. If he hadn't stepped in, how far would this abuse have gone?

Ask your child "What will you do when somebody bullies you?" Discuss with your child her options and appropriate actions when bullying occurs. Your child needs to know that it is important to report the bullying immediately, to nip it in the bud.

If you detect bullying of any kind, here are some actions that are helpful:

- Go immediately to other parents, school authorities, and adults. The victim needs an adult in his or her corner. Our children are not equipped to handle these situations (and some adults aren't either).
- Do not sweep it under the rug! Parents and leaders need to be honest when it comes to any act of bullying, no matter how big or small.

- Teach the bullies how their actions harm others.
- If your child is being bullied, ask yourself: "Is my child doing anything to provoke bullying? Is she fueling the fire?" No victim deserves abuse, but children must be taught how not to engage.
- If your child is the bully, try to determine if this is a cry for help, or an expression of other insecurities that you need to address.

If you detect Facebook bullying, you may:

1. Report the offender to Facebook.
2. Block them as a Facebook Friend.

On Facebook, the most efficient way to report abuse is to do it in the same place it occurs. This means that if you or your child receives a harassing message in your Inbox, you can report the message by clicking on the "Report" link next to the sender's name. If the person is a Facebook Friend, you can remove that person as a Friend by clicking on the "Remove" link as well as the "Report" link. Facebook states that reporting the message as harassment will automatically add this person to your Block list.

Every message sent on Facebook identifies the sender. If you click the name, you will go to the abuser's Profile, where you will find the "Report/Block person" link that appears at the bottom of that person's Profile. If abusive messages continue even after you've blocked them, you can ask a friend to also report them to Facebook. Reports are confidential and the user being reported does not know that they have been reported. After a report is submitted, Facebook will investigate the issue and determine whether the content should remain on the site based on their Terms of Service. As Facebook states:

"Cyberbullies usually seek a reaction from the people they harass. When they fail to get one, they often give up gradually. Rather than responding to a bully via Inbox, a Wall post, or Facebook Chat, you can delete offensive posts from your Wall or messages from your Inbox and then use the "Block" or "Report" functions to resolve the issue safely. To delete an offensive Wall post, hover over the post in question, click the "Remove" button that appears, and select "Delete" in the dialogue box. To delete a message from Inbox, simply click the "Delete" button at the top of the message. Only confirmed friends can post to your Wall or send you a message through Chat. If you are receiving posts and Chat messages you don't like, you should consider removing the sender from your friends list."

By being aware of the causes and not just the results of bullying, we get the opportunity to address these problems at the root level. The old adage of "An ounce of prevention is worth a pound of cure" certainly applies with the issue of bullying, whether it is on the Internet or in real life.

References

Below are helpful websites for more information, tools, and resources on cyberbullying:
• stopcyberbullying.org
• connectsafely.org
• connectsafely.org/Safety-Tips/tips-to-help-stop-cyberbullying.html
• www.pluk.org/Pubs/Bullying2.pdf
• stopcyberbullying.org/prevention/index.html

Who owns the content posted to Facebook?

Name:	BJ Fogg
Websites:	http://bjfogg.com
	http://captology.stanford.edu

Last summer I gathered with my extended family in Idaho for a reunion. I snapped a photo of my mom cooking fish, and I uploaded the shot to Facebook, creating a new album. I forgot about this photo until months later. I then noticed that this photo was shared with "Everyone," the default setting on Facebook. I had forgotten to change the privacy settings for the new album.

Ugh. That wasn't what I wanted. By using Facebook to share this image with "Everyone," I had granted Facebook broad rights to use the fish photo in many ways. Although I doubt Facebook would exploit my mom's cooking to advertise fish, they would have that right.

Bloggers and journalists freaked out in early 2009 when Facebook revised its Terms of Service.[1] The headlines screamed that Facebook was staking claim to anything you shared on their site. The blog posts and articles pointed out that Facebook would have this right forever, even if you deleted your account.

Parents may think of themselves as behind the times with Facebook, but they were way ahead on this issue. Even before this controversy erupted, parents often asked us this question: "Who owns what gets posted to Facebook?"

The short answer is: You own what you post on Facebook, but at the same time Facebook often gains some rights to what you post. The surprising part is that the rights you give to Facebook can be pretty broad, including using your content for advertising or commercial purposes. And this is why bloggers and journalists sounded an alarm on the new terms Facebook rolled out in 2009. It seemed that Facebook could even use your child's photo to make a profit.

Frankly, most users don't care about Facebook's terms. And teens especially seem uninterested in the legal issues around Facebook. But this makes it all the more important for parents to understand ownership of Facebook content.

Facebook's current Terms of Service say:

"You grant us a non-exclusive, transferable, sub-licensable, royalty-free, worldwide license to use any IP content that you post on or in connection with Facebook."

This means that what you upload or type into Facebook (your "IP content") gets licensed to Facebook, to use as they see fit in operating their service.

For those who want to read the detailed legal language, check out the paragraph below:

"You hereby grant Facebook an irrevocable, perpetual, non-exclusive, transferable, fully paid, worldwide license (with the right to sublicense) to (a) use, copy, publish, stream, store, retain, publicly perform or display, transmit, scan, reformat, modify,

edit, frame, translate, excerpt, adapt, create derivative works and distribute (through multiple tiers), any User Content you Post on or in connection with the Facebook Service or the promotion thereof subject only to your privacy settings or[2] enable a user to Post, including by offering a Share Link on your website and (b) to use your name, likeness and image for any purpose, including commercial or advertising, each of (a) and (b) on or in connection with the Facebook Service or the promotion thereof." [2]

In our view, Facebook is not being sneaky or devious. We don't believe there's a conspiracy to use family reunion photos to sell fish—or anything like that. Instead, Facebook is doing what's necessary to run their service. As we see it, if Facebook did not have rights to share what you posted, such as a photo, then the service couldn't share your content with friends. There have to be some legal terms that allow sharing.

As Facebook's Mark Zuckerberg describes it:

"Our philosophy is that people own their information and control who they share it with. When a person shares information on Facebook, they first need to grant Facebook a license to use that information so that we can show it to the other people they've asked us to share it with." [3]

That said, parents are right to be concerned about who really owns the content posted to Facebook. What happens when families face off with Facebook lawyers over some issue that pits privacy against profit? The destiny of digital content in the decades to come is unclear—be it email, YouTube videos, or Facebook comments. But spending time wringing our hands over what might happen is sort of useless. Instead, I want to focus on two key issues that are here today and actionable for parents.

First of all, Facebook's license is limited by your privacy settings. This fact has been mostly overlooked (or ignored) by bloggers and journalists. Facebook makes this point clear early on in their Terms of Service:

> *"You own all of the content and information you post on Facebook, and you can control how it is shared through your privacy and application settings."*

That means if you use Facebook tools to restrict who can see what you post, then Facebook can't use that content broadly. If I had uploaded the photo of my Mom cooking fish and allowed only Friends to view it, then Facebook's future use of that photo would be restricted.

In order to claim ownership of our Facebook information, we need to take that extra step. Otherwise, Facebook can use it. Remember: In many cases, the default is set to share with "Everybody."

The message here is a major theme of our work with parents: Get to know the privacy settings on Facebook. Make these settings a topic of discussion with your family. Don't accept the default settings. In other words, take control of who has access to what you do on Facebook.

As Facebook points out:

> *"When you publish content or information using the 'Everyone' setting, it means that everyone, including people off of Facebook, will have access to that information and we may not have control over what they do with it."*

The next issue is about removing content from Facebook. Yes, you can delete photos, comments, and so on. That's your right.

And when you delete content, Facebook's license to it also gets removed, unless you've shared the content with others. Consider the following example to clarify.

Let's suppose that after I posted the photo of my Mom cooking fish, my Aunt Beverly sees the photo and decides to post it on her Facebook profile page, with her own comment: *"The classic family fish recipe!"*

If I delete that fish photo, will my Aunt Beverly lose the image as well? Facebook has decided that the answer is no. I cannot delete content I've shared in this way with others. And when you think about it, this approach makes sense. If I had sent Aunt Bev an email, would I be able to delete it later? Facebook applies the same logic to all their content.

At the end of the day, Facebook is in business to make money. On one hand, the more content people share openly, the more valuable Facebook becomes. On the other hand, Facebook is working to maintain the trust of their users, which includes allowing them to control their own content. These two forces—profit and trust—seem to be in opposition at times. Specifically, the Facebook interface is designed, by default, to encourage broad sharing of the content you post. But at the same time, you can take control of your content by using the privacy settings.

Your challenge as a Facebook parent is to inspire your kids to care enough to do the extra work of controlling their content.

References

1 http://www.securityfocus.com/columnists/497
   http://www.facebook.com/group.php?v=info&gid=62447246097
   http://consumerist.com/2009/02/facebooks-new-terms-of-service-we-can-do-anything-
   we-want-with-your-content-forever.html

2 http://www.facebook.com/terms.php

3 http://blog.facebook.com/blog.php?post=54434097130

Can Facebook ruin my child's chances for a top college?

Name:	BJ Fogg
Websites:	http://bjfogg.com
	http://captology.stanford.edu

I have a niece who hopes to attend a top-tier university, like Stanford or MIT. She's big on using Facebook, and she's friended me. As a result, I can see what she posts. Once in a while, I see a post that makes me cringe. At those moments, I feel like texting her urgently: "Hey, you should delete that silly post! Bad judgment." But I've done this only once. All other times, I've simply clicked away to other Facebook pages.

Will my niece's use of Facebook affect her chances at a top university?

Facebook will affect her college prospects. However, the impact is not what most parents expect.

In our work with parents, Linda and I find that many wonder if college admissions offices use Facebook to determine which students to reject and accept, like Santa Claus making a list of naughty and nice. It's an easy picture to imagine: people in suits, sitting in a university office, surfing Facebook, looking for condemning evidence against each applicant.

That's just not the case. I have yet to find any evidence that admissions teams at top universities are using Facebook to unearth teenage foibles. That's why I don't worry so much about my niece. She may not always present her best self on Facebook, but her lapses will not be headline news for people evaluating her college application.

Yes, it is true that more and more admissions offices are using Facebook (a recent study puts the figure at 29%).[1] However, the offices use Facebook to recruit students, not to disqualify them. That's an important twist to the image most parents have in mind. And this means parents need a new view of Facebook's impact on college admissions. If your child is not learning about colleges by using Facebook, she is missing an excellent source of information.

In the U.S., millions of high school students use Facebook. This includes the teens universities want most—smart, motivated, talented. So it only makes sense that colleges are reaching out to prospective students using Facebook.

Admissions officers post to Facebook, and they answer questions. It can be personal and direct. In the future, in efforts to recruit the best and brightest candidates, universities will organize events via Facebook and even create Facebook apps. Stanford is already well down this path.

Why wouldn't colleges want Facebook-savvy students? Social networking is a skill. To increase that skill, teens must practice. And the best place today to practice is on Facebook. What your child learns about using Facebook effectively will help her for the rest of her life, including in college admissions.

Consider leadership skills as one example. Teenagers can learn how to use Facebook to benefit charitable causes or address social issues. Your child can start a Facebook Group, build a Fan Page, organize an event—all of this via Facebook. In the future, leadership will require an ability to engage your social network and lead teams that are virtual.

Imagine how impressive it would be to learn about a teenager who has used Facebook to organize 50,000 people for a cause. Or even just 500 people. With Facebook and the right skills, this kind of feat has been achieved by teens. And this impact will impress admissions officers, who are looking for the leaders of the future.

So when it comes to Facebook, Linda and I emphasize its positive aspects for teens. They can learn leadership, empathy, collaboration, self-presentation, and more. But kids won't learn these skills very well without coaches. And that's where parents come in. Parents who understand the positive potential of Facebook can better guide their kids towards being effective leaders and skilled collaborators. They certainly aren't teaching this stuff in high schools (yet). We urge you not to miss this opportunity to be a Facebook guide.

Social networking is here to stay, even if Facebook dies off. Knowing how to use social networks effectively is a vital skill for teens now and for their success in the future.

Can Facebook put skeletons in my child's closet?

So far my answers to this chapter's question have been upbeat. I now offer another answer—the worrisome response you may have expected. Yes, Facebook can put skeletons in your child's closet.

Even though the top colleges are not using Facebook to dig up dirt on applicants, what teens do on Facebook can hurt them in other areas. For example, when my class at Stanford has too many students attending on the first day, I have to cut some students. I use Facebook to help me decide which students will benefit most from what I teach.

In a professional setting, I use Facebook as one way to decide whom I hire to work with me. I'm not the only one.[2] I consider this part of my due diligence. If someone's Profile is not accessible to strangers, that's good. If I can access an applicant's Profile, and I see junky things, then I'm not impressed. I won't hire that person. Why? Because people who work with me need excellent judgment.

There may come a time when admissions officers look to Facebook to determine judgment and character of applicants, but that day is not yet here. And if your child has judgment, they won't allow strangers—including those at Stanford or Harvard—to view their Profile Page on Facebook. Smart applicants will know how to use Facebook privacy settings.

References

1 Nora Ganim Barnes and Eric Mattson, 2009. "Social Media and College Admissions: The First Longitudinal Study," Studies and Research, Center for Marketing Research, University of Massachusetts, Dartmouth, http://www.umassd.edu/cmr/studiesresearch/mediaandadmissions.cfm.

2 http://www.businessweek.com/bschools/content/sep2008/bs20080928_509398.htm

3 http://gigaom.com/2010/01/27/yes-virginia-hr-execs-check-your-facebook-page/ and http://www.microsoft.com/privacy/dpd/research.aspx

What if my kids won't friend me?

| Name: | Linda Fogg Phillips |
| Websites: | www.FacebookForParents.org |

When I first joined Facebook, I caught my children off guard. Out of the blue I popped up on Facebook, requesting to be their Friend. My kids had no idea that I had even considered getting my own account. I was sitting at my desk one evening, just friending away, systematically sending requests to each of my children.

By joining Facebook, I was pioneering new territory in parenting. "Where there is potential for danger, Mom will be there," I thought. My daughter, McCall, was sitting in a nearby room using her laptop. All of a sudden she exclaimed from the other room:

"Oh, Mom! That is just weird!"

Ha ha! She was on Facebook and had just discovered my Friend request.

She came running into my office with an offended look on her face, "What are you doing on Facebook?! That is just weird!"

I just sat at my desk looking at her with a big smile on my face, like the cat who just swallowed the canary. "So, are you going to friend me?" I asked with a chuckle.

"Nobody else's mom is on Facebook! That is just weird!" she repeated for the third time.

The next 24 hours were entertaining for me, as each of my children logged onto their Facebook accounts to discover me waiting to be "confirmed" or "denied." I tried to be inconspicuously present as they logged onto Facebook, anticipating their reactions like an excited hostess before a surprise party. The puzzled expressions on their faces when they saw I was hiding among their new Friend requests were priceless. They would glance up at me from their computers, and I would just smile back.

Some time has passed since I first friended my kids. Back then, teens and college students alike threatened to abandon Facebook if parents were allowed. The resistance has died down, and kids now accept that they have to share their playground with the bigger kids on the block—their parents.

I was puzzled by parents in our first Stanford "Facebook for Parents" class who would say, "My child won't friend me." My initial response to this was, "What? Don't you provide food, clothing and shelter for this child? Don't you drive this child around for endless hours every week? Don't you cater to her every need? And you say she won't friend you?"

To me, the solution seemed obvious—you must insist your child friend you on Facebook. But I would soon learn a better way.

At the conclusion of our second class, one mom reluctantly approached me. Her name was Annette. I was hastily gathering our class materials in order to catch my flight back home to Las Vegas as I looked up from the table at the front of our classroom and saw her patiently waiting for me to notice her.

"Can I talk to you for a minute?" she said.

"Sure." I stopped and gave her my full attention.

"My daughter won't friend me," she said hesitantly. "What

do I do? I'm really worried about her. She's at that age when kids don't want to have their parents telling them what to do."

Annette continued, "She is always on Facebook. I have no idea what she is doing or who she is talking to on Facebook. She hardly ever talks to me or tells me anything about what's going on with her. She's going through a rebellious stage right now. I'm worried." Her voice started to crack as tears filled her eyes. "I'm afraid that if I tell her she must be my Friend on Facebook, she will completely shut me out. What do I do?"

For a moment I was at a loss for words. I could feel this mother's concern and pain. I suddenly did not feel qualified to give her any advice. My heart was breaking for her. As I stood there for a moment praying in my heart to know how to respond, the answer came to me clear as day.

"Annette, just be patient," I said. "Your daughter knows that you love her and are concerned about her. She may never want you to be her Friend on Facebook, and that's okay. Just keep working on being her friend in real life."

For the next few weeks of class, Annette sought me out afterwards and gave me updates on her own progress in learning to use Facebook. She said that her daughter was intrigued that her mother was learning how to navigate this new world, yet she was still not willing to friend her.

On the night of our last class, Annette once again approached me as had been the pattern, only this time it was before class started. She had a gleam in her eye as she exclaimed, "My daughter finally friended me! She has finally let me into a part of her life that I have felt so shut out of."

Not every "non-friending" situation ends up like Annette's. But that's okay. Your efforts to become familiar with Facebook will show your child that you care about what they are doing, that you are interested in their life.

I watched other parents in our classes whose children wouldn't friend them on Facebook. As I saw them struggling with this issue, I gained empathy for the uniqueness of each situation. This changed me.

I realized that every family was different, with a different set of values. Of course, I knew this before I started teaching, but I finally embraced this reality deeply. Who was I to say what was right and wrong for each family? With this principle in mind, we hope to empower you with enough insight into Facebook so that you can apply what you learn to your family, according to your own values and dynamics.

Facebook is not our old world. College students created it to connect with their peers. In many ways this online service has changed the power dynamics between parents and children. That is not to say parents are not empowered by Facebook. It simply means that our kids got there first. Now it's our job to catch up as fast as possible and be parents in the new world, too.

How do I fit in on Facebook?

Name: **Linda Fogg Phillips**
Websites: **www.FacebookForParents.org**

Fear is the #1 reason most kids don't want their parents on Facebook. They are afraid that you, despite your best intentions, will embarrass them. This may surprise you, but that's what our research suggests. Of course, most parents think "spying" is why kids shiver at the thought of parents online. That's not the case. What kids fear most is looking bad to their peers. This concern isn't new. Remember when your child insisted that you drop her off at the end of the street after you chauffeured her to school? She probably didn't want you doing anything at the school gate that might jeopardize her social standing.

So how do you overcome this concern?

Facebook is a unique culture with its own language. If you learn the culture and language, you are less likely to embarrass your children. And deep down, your child probably knows this: The smarter you are about Facebook, the better you'll behave online. But as you are toddling forward, kids worry about the parental growing pains that they must endure.

Learning the culture of Facebook takes time. Until you have a better grasp, you may want to refer to the handy list of things NOT to post on Facebook:

- a lists of chores
- your opinions about your children's music
- your daughter's photo as a baby on the potty
- comments on boyfriends/girlfriends
- every worry that pops into your mind
- photos of your son crying on Santa's lap
- nags longer than ten words
- lectures longer than zero words
- any photo your teen did not pre-approve (including photos of you)
- scolds of your children's friends
- typing LOL after statements that are not funny
- requests for emoticon translation
- Friend requests to the children of parents you met at the PTA meeting
- reminders that you've read this book

Believe it or not, I have seen parents post all of these things on Facebook, except the last one. With all of this parental misbehavior, is it any wonder that teenagers are afraid to friend their parents?

In teaching parents about Facebook, we saw this pattern: As parents used Facebook with their own circle of friends, kids got more comfortable in friending them. And to our surprise, parents reported that at times, it was the child who initiated the Friend request. (Yes, parents were ecstatic when this happened.)

Here are the steps you can take to become Facebook fluent, as you strive to earn the trust and confidence of your child as a Facebook Friend.

Step 1: Friend your relatives

First of all, start your Facebook life by friending family members, both immediate and extended. You may even find some long lost relatives! Facebook often reunites family members who have been out of touch for years.

You can use Facebook to search for family members by entering their names in the "search" box at the top part of any page. Once you find a few roots to your family tree, you simply follow these roots. Suppose you find your cousin, Reed, on Facebook. You then click to see Reed's Friends. If you know any of them (and you probably will), invite those people to be your Friend on Facebook. Most of them will accept in a day or two. Soon your tree will grow branches and sprout leaves before your very eyes.

Once your relatives are your Facebook Friends, you are now in the game. You can watch what others post and see how people respond. We find that parents are hesitant to post at first—even a simple status update can be intimidating. The fix is to just dive in. Update your status, comment on a photo, and even post your own photos (choose wisely!). Besides learning about Facebook's culture, you'll see how easy it is to stay aware of the important (and not so important) happenings in the lives of your relatives. And they can stay current with you too.

Step 2: Friend your own friends

The next step is to friend your real-life friends. You'll be surprised at how many of your old friends and acquaintances are already on Facebook. You can search out friends by high school or college. Just like before, once you find someone you know, you simply follow the trail to more people you know. Let's suppose you find your old roommate Jeannie. When you click to see Jeannie's Friends on Facebook, you'll likely see some people you know. You'll be connecting and reuniting with people whom you haven't heard from in years. (Word of caution here: We suggest long-lost boyfriends and girlfriends stay that way. They were lost for a reason.)

Besides finding long-lost friends, you should search for current friends, such as neighbors, tennis partners, and people from your church. I'm always surprised at how much I learn about my real-life friends on Facebook. You may think you know your hairdresser well, but just wait until you start reading her posts on Facebook. It's a whole new level of insight. This will give you a glimpse into the power of Facebook to create new channels for building relationships.

Along the way, as you connect with relatives and real-world friends, you'll gain more confidence with Facebook. And you'll get more insight into the culture and etiquette of this online world.

Step 3: Attempt to friend your child (again)

Now that you have your own set of Friends on Facebook, you can try again to friend your children. At this point, they know you're not a complete newbie.

If your kids don't accept your friending request, don't give up! Keep trying every so often. I predict the time will come that your child will press "Accept," and you will be counted among her Friends on Facebook. Hooray. By accepting you as a Friend, she's trusting that you'll behave nicely in her world. I hope this book will help you be a model citizen.

Some parents—but not all—may be more inclined to take a more assertive approach to friending their children. I have a policy that all our children under 18 must be my Friend on Facebook. Yes, sometimes I am met with resistance, but I feel that this policy is no different from when they use my car: I want to know where they are going and when to expect them home.

I interact with each of my children on Facebook differently.

With one of them, I am merely a shadow, invisible to her network. She hates when I post things her Friends can see. So I respect that. In contrast, my other children interact with me frequently by posting on my Wall and vice versa. And that's a lot of fun.

I admit, how we use Facebook at my home may seem strange. Sometimes my children and I will be sitting in the same room, each with our own laptops, and we are connecting only through Facebook. We are carrying on a lively conversation by posting on each other's Walls and making comments. At times, we'll all burst out in sudden laughter, without a word spoken. An outside observer would never have a clue as to what just happened.

Being a Facebook Friend with my children has brought a new dimension to our relationships. We are more present in each other's lives. This is a technology that I love because it has strengthened my relationship with my children in a way that I would have never dreamed possible.

How do I contact Facebook about a problem?

Name:	BJ Fogg
Websites:	http://bjfogg.com
	http://captology.stanford.edu

A distressed parent emailed me a few months ago.

Someone had started a Fan Page on Facebook in the name of her daughter, Beatrice. The Page was filled with images and comments saying that Beatrice was a good source for drugs. The parent explained that even though this was false, the kids at Beatrice's high school knew all about the Page. The parent desperately wanted my advice: How could she stop people from using Facebook to trash her daughter, Beatrice?

I logged into Facebook and found the renegade Fan Page. I saw that a few hundred people were Fans. A few dozen had posted comments on the Page, describing the drugs they got from Beatrice and telling stories of her wanton ways. The Page read like an endorsement for Beatrice's drug dealership.

This was the first time I'd seen a Fan Page being used to tear down a teen's reputation. I was saddened that someone would create such a Page, and that so many teens would become Fans. I knew that damage had been done to Beatrice and her family. But

I also knew that by taking the right steps, the parent and Beatrice could put an end to this fiasco.

Let's suppose that something terrible happens on Facebook: Someone posts a photo of your daughter nude, a bully creates a Facebook Group to harm minorities, or someone has hacked into your Facebook account and sent fake messages asking for money from your Friends. What can you do?

Although extremely bad things are uncommon on Facebook, Linda and I have seen all of the above happen. When things go terribly wrong on Facebook, you can't always just delete the photo or close down the offensive Group by yourself.

We've been surprised at how often people have reached out to us, as teachers of "Facebook for Parents," hoping we could connect them to staffers at Facebook who would then fix their terrible problem. These requests led us to write this chapter. We hope you never need to use this information, but if you do someday, remember to come back here and follow our advice.

When things go wrong on Facebook, I suggest you follow these steps:

Step 1: Document the problem

The first step is to make a record of what is wrong. Ideally, you would capture an image of the screen, called a "screenshot," to document the problem in a concrete, visual way. Most computers have built-in software to take screenshots. (If you need help, look up "screenshot" on Wikipedia for guidance.)

Next, you should write down the date, people involved, and so on. Make a record of what you did to solve the problem, when it occurred, and who was involved. In the best case, you'll never need to use your documentation, but the few minutes you spend capturing the problem may be vital later.

Step 2: Use Facebook's built-in system for solving problems

Facebook has a good system for reporting problems with Groups, Apps, and other aspects of their site. To find the "Report" link, look in the lower part of the left-hand column of any Group or Page. This then brings up an interface to categorize the problem.

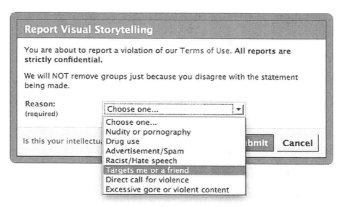

The reporting link for Photos is different. When you're viewing Photos on Facebook, right below the photo is a link where you can report it as inappropriate. The same is true for Videos, Notes, Events, and more.

If you cannot find a built-in way to report the problem, then go on to Step 3.

Step 3: Email abuse@facebook.com

We hope you can solve your problem before reaching Step 3. But sometimes you may not find a built-in system for reporting a problem. For example, there is no way to automatically report a

threatening status update or a comment. In such cases, you'll need to use Facebook's Help system. Here's how: On every Facebook page you'll find a "Help Center" link at the bottom right. Clicking "Help Center" brings up a range of options. Look for the one that fits your concern.

On the main Help page, you'll find a tab that says "Safety." At that page (http://www.facebook.com/safety/) you'll find out how Facebook handles issues:

Despite Facebook's safety and privacy controls, Facebook cannot guarantee that the site is entirely free of illegal, offensive, pornographic or otherwise inappropriate material, or that its members will not encounter inappropriate or illegal conduct from other members. Consequently, you may encounter such content and conduct. You can help Facebook by notifying us of any nudity, pornography, harassment or unwelcome contact by clicking on the "Report" link located on pages throughout the site. Facebook will use its best efforts to review reports made through this site reporting tool within 24 hours and remove any content that is deemed to have violated the Statement of Rights and Responsibilities. If warranted Facebook will also warn or disable the user responsible for posting the abusive content. Where complaints about nudity, pornography, harassment or unwelcome contact are made by independent email to abuse@facebook.com, Facebook will acknowledge receipt of the complaint and begin to address it within 24 hours. Facebook will respond to the reporter within 72 hours of receiving the email complaint to inform them of the steps Facebook has taken to address it.

A few things to note from Facebook's stated policy above:

A. You can email your problem to abuse@facebook.com
B. Facebook will try to review your report within 24 hours
C. Facebook will report back to you within 72 hours

In our view, Facebook has done good work improving their system for reporting problems. As you look over the options given at their Safety pages, you'll see a thorough list of issues. What other website offers such easy and clear safety instructions? Good for Facebook! Their help system was once not so swift, but they've stepped up, and we want to give them credit for the improvement.

Phoning or visiting Facebook is not useful

We've found that parents sometimes want to phone Facebook to resolve their problem. The fact is that phone calls don't work. We've seen the futility of this approach.

During our research visits to Facebook, we've sat in the headquarter lobby waiting for our appointments. While there, we've watched the receptionist take phone call after phone call, referring everyone back to the website. We asked one receptionist about this process. She says she never patches people with problems through to a live person. That's a big part of her job: To get people to use

Facebook's online help system.

This seems the only reasonable approach. Facebook has hundreds of millions of users. They have only a few hundred employees. They have no phone support and no way to resolve issues via phone. And you can't really show up in the main lobby and get your problem solved either. That's not how Facebook works. But if against all odds you want to try these ways of resolving your issue, below you'll find the company information:

Facebook Headquarters
1601 S. California Ave.
Palo Alto, CA 94304
Phone: 650-543-4800
Fax: 650-543-4801

Resources
For more about Facebook, Inc.: http://www.crunchbase.com/company/facebook
Safety resources on Facebook: http://www.facebook.com/safety/

How do I stay current with Facebook?

Name:	BJ Fogg
Websites:	http://bjfogg.com
	http://captology.stanford.edu

If you've read this far, you're probably serious about Facebook. Good for you! The more you use Facebook, the more you'll learn about how it works, the more fun you'll have—and the less concern you'll have about your child spending time in this new world.

The fact is that few users learn everything about Facebook. This service offers so many options, from Apps to Friend Lists to Events. Plus, it's difficult to master Facebook when the service changes so often. Like a good Internet company, Facebook continues to evolve. You should expect changes in the interface, the policies, in how friending works, and more.

In the past, whenever Facebook made changes, people complained. Someone would always start a protest group on Facebook, such as "Bring Back the Old Facebook!" But after a few weeks of clamor and media coverage, the protestors calmed down. Most people realized that the changes were improvements. For example, when Facebook added the News Feed in 2006, college students protested loudly. But today, the News Feed is perhaps the most used and most loved feature in Facebook.

If you, as a parent, stay current with the changes in Facebook—what's new, what's popular, what's the latest controversy—you'll find three benefits.

Benefit #1: Your child will be impressed

Imagine yourself at the dinner table telling your daughter about the results of Facebook's latest hackathon. Your daughter will be amazed you even know what that is.

Benefit #2: You won't get confused

If the history of Facebook is any guide, the Facebook system you use today will look different a year from now. Usually these changes are announced before they are rolled out. So if you stay current, using our steps below, you'll usually learn about the changes before they happen. Then you won't be confused when you log on and things look different. You'll take it all in stride.

Benefit #3: You'll be able to keep family members safer

When something big changes in Facebook, it's a good time to scrutinize your privacy settings. Why? Because I've found that sometimes the settings revert to the default after the Facebook interface undergoes a redesign. Facebook has since improved their technology, so I don't think your settings will unexpectedly revert in the future, but it's not impossible.

To keep you on the cutting edge of Facebook, I suggest five methods. If you adopt even two of the methods below, you will likely know more about Facebook than your child. And that, I think, is a good thing for any parent.

Method 1. Use Facebook often, but not all the time

The first method for staying current with Facebook is to use the service frequently. I'm not proposing you hang out on Facebook for hours. Just log on for five minutes a day. That's all you need. How do I know? In our Facebook class at Stanford, we asked half the parents to use Facebook for four minutes a day. After six weeks, the "four-minutes-for-Facebook" parents showed remarkable growth in Facebook savviness. In fact, we measured their progress in 10 ways. And in all 10 ways, parents benefited. In my opinion, spending five minutes a day using Facebook is better than cramming five hours in a binge session.

Method 2. Read Facebook's official blog

You may think the official Facebook blog would be just a bunch of PR pablum. But the actual blog may surprise you. Give it at least one shot and read a few posts. You'll see that the topics range from Gifts to Games, Privacy to Parents. And you'll see that almost 200 different staffers have written helpful tips and techniques for the blog. It's not just a PR person pumping out "feel good" prose. To me, the Facebook blog feels like a grown-up "show and tell." The employees who are creating and improving Facebook are the ones who write the posts, telling you about what they've done as if you are a trusted friend. It gives you a real feel for the down-to-earth people behind Facebook.

You'll find it at blog.facebook.com.

Method 3: Read the unofficial Facebook blogs

If you want to get an outsider's perspective on Facebook, you have some excellent choices. My favorites are:
- http://www.allfacebook.com/
- http://www.insidefacebook.com/
- http://mashable.com/category/facebook/

At these sites you'll find smart, concise explanations of what's happening with Facebook by people who are not paid by Facebook.

Nick O'Neil writes AllFacebook. Nick is so knowledgeable. I think he must use Facebook all day, every day. When something changes at Facebook, Nick will tell you right away, explaining it in terms that normal people can understand.

Inside Facebook by Justin Smith is for marketers and entrepreneurs who want to use Facebook to sell products. Even if you're not creating a Facebook app, you can learn about how the business world on Facebook works by reading Justin's posts.

Mashable has a broader focus. Think Wall Street Journal for digital media. For example, when Bill Gates finally joined Twitter, Mashable covered it with flair. The section about Facebook is consistently strong.

Method 4. Our website & newsletter

At our own website and in our newsletter, Linda and I explain Facebook issues that matter most to parents. Our periodic newsletter offers headlines and short articles. The website itself features videos and resources to help you learn and stay current with Facebook. See: www.FacebookForParents.org

Method 5. Google alert for Facebook

The fifth and final method we suggest to stay current with Facebook comes to you courtesy of Google. If you haven't yet started using Google Alerts, read on. Almost every time I introduce somebody to Google Alerts, they thank me later.

Google has created an alert service that will automatically email you short segments of all the newest stuff on whatever topic you choose. For example, I set up an alert for "Persuasive Technology Lab," which is my research lab at Stanford. Every day

I get an email from Google that links me to anything new on the Internet about my lab. It's the easiest way for me to keep up.

I have an alert for "Facebook." In my daily email from Google on all things Facebook, I usually have about 20 items. I scan the headlines. Usually I click on two or three things to read more. I suggest you set up a Google Alert for Facebook and any other topic or organization that matters to you. It's one of Google's best services.

http://www.google.com/alerts

Staying Facebook-hip doesn't require a lot of time. It requires consistency. The Facebook world seems to change every day. After a while, you'll get accustomed to the types and rhythm of the changes. When something breaks the patterns, you'll spot it. And you'll be able to take steps early to benefit your family and yourself.

Facebook is not a fad. It's not going away. The more you learn now, the better adapted you'll be for what comes next. Soon you may find yourself advising your friends who didn't see the importance of Facebook as early as you did. Eventually, I believe you'll be guiding your children through this new realm with a parent's experience and wisdom.

How can I use Facebook as a parenting tool?

Name: **Linda Fogg Phillips**
Websites: **www.FacebookForParents.org**

Have you ever wished you were more in tune with your children? Had more insight into their needs, not just their wants? Had a crystal ball that could tell you what they were thinking? Kids are often difficult to figure out. You ask them a question and you feel lucky if you get more than a shrug, yet they could spend hours on Facebook or the phone if you let them.

In many ways, Facebook is the tool parents have dreamed of. In fact, I call it the "Power Tool of Parenting."

What kind of tools does a carpenter use to build a house? In the "olden days" his primary tools would be a handsaw, a screwdriver, and a hammer. In our lifetime, the carpenter has upgraded to the more efficient tools of a power saw, an electric screw gun, and a pneumatic nailer. As we build and help our children develop, we need to upgrade our parenting tools to more efficient power tools as well.

Facebook is one of the most powerful tools available to parents in this decade. I have taken some heat and criticism for making such a bold statement, but after a lot of research and experience on Facebook, I deeply believe in and stand behind this claim. Whether or not you like Facebook, it can be used in either a positive or negative way in your parenting. The choice is yours. The effectiveness of Facebook as a parenting tool, like the tools a carpenter uses, depends on the skill and knowledge of the user.

Let's get to the nuts and bolts about why Facebook is the Power Tool of Parenting and how it can assist us.

1. Be more aware

If you were listening in on the parent-to-parent phone conversation I had with Jane one evening, you would have understood why I was in an awkward spot.

"Jane, I don't want to stick my nose where it doesn't belong," I said, "but Jared posted something on Facebook that has me a bit concerned and I thought that you might want to know."

At the time, Jane did not have a Facebook account. Jared was her seventeen-year-old son. He was my daughter's Facebook Friend, and he had invited me to be his Friend as well.

It is not uncommon for kids to express feelings on their Walls that they do not yet have the ability to express verbally. Jared's post was such: "I hate my life. I am done. I don't want to be here any more. Nobody cares and nobody will miss me."

As Jared's status update came into my News Feed, I sat there looking at it, frozen in time. I must have sat there for several minutes, with all the possible scenarios of what it could mean running through my head.

"Oh, I'm sure it's nothing," I thought as I brushed it off. I got up from my desk and proceeded to fix dinner for my family. Thirty minutes went by. "Nobody cares, nobody will miss me" still echoed in my head.

If my child typed such a thing into Facebook, would I want

another parent to inform me?

I decided that I would risk damaging my friendship with Jane, just in case there was more meaning to Jared's post than I wanted to believe.

I phoned her. The conversation with Jane went much better than expected. She was sincerely appreciative that I cared enough about her son to go out on a limb and call it to her attention.

"Jared has been a bit depressed lately," she explained, "but I was not aware that it had gotten to this point."

By the end of that night, Jane had set up her own Facebook account and friended all three of her children.

That day, Jane realized the powerful tool that Facebook could be for her as a parent. She realized Facebook added unprecedented insight into the needs of her children. Facebook does not replace the essential personal interaction that we need to have with our children, but it can be one of the best power tools that we have. It allows us to continue to build and strengthen our relationships with them. When we have increased awareness, we increase our ability to meet their needs.

2. Communicate better

The ability to communicate better with my kids is the one thing I like most about Facebook. The following example, a series of posts from my daughter's Wall, shows how powerful a tool Facebook is in that respect.

Danielle Phillips ask me something:)

 Linda Fogg Phillips Can you come help me clean my closet?

 Danielle Phillips no.

 Linda Fogg Phillips You said to ask you something ;)

 Danielle Phillips don't make me de-friend you..

 Linda Fogg Phillips wanna go get some hot chocolate with me or something?

 Danielle Phillips Haha are you upstairs? And sure that sounds good

 Linda Fogg Phillips yes - let's go!

A minute later, my fifteen-year-old daughter laughingly ran up the stairs to my room to get me for a hot chocolate run. We were able to spend 30 minutes of one-on-one time together. Facebook was a virtual bridge into my daughter's real life world!

Next, consider the case of Tom, my friend who has a son living in Australia. After a divorce, Tom moved to the United States, but his son stayed in Australia to become a professional surfer. Tom and his son became estranged for several years. Tom set up a Facebook account for the sole purpose of finding his son. He was elated when his son accepted his Friend request. They were finally reconnected. Today, Tom communicates with his son mostly through Facebook.

3. Teach life skills

Parents can use Facebook to help teach their kids some important life skills. This positive side of Facebook often gets overlooked. BJ and I think this perspective matters. We see savvy parents using Facebook as a way to coach their kids in five areas:

Leadership skills

The features in Facebook allow teens to create groups, publicize events and generate support for causes. These are important leadership skills, but kids won't learn these skills simply because Facebook has some nice features. The experience that parents have with leadership in the pre-Facebook world can be applied to what teens can do online. The key is to adapt your leadership experience to work with the tools Facebook offers.

Professional skills

Your teen may not be thinking very much about her career right now, but her activities on Facebook can help her build professional skills. For example, the ability to collaborate remotely will be vital in the future. Facebook is an excellent training ground. Other skills include presenting information and giving feedback to others on their ideas. Isn't this what teens are doing on Facebook already? That's good news. Again, teens won't magically learn these skills without mentors. They are learning, and you can help, drawing on your own experience.

Learning skills

Two important learning skills are critical thinking and adapting to change. Facebook is an environment to practice both. When your child's Friends post things online, from simple Status Update to long Notes, your child is naturally assessing the accuracy and worth of each item. Sure, the content on Facebook may be mostly social; it's not serious academic stuff. Even so, critical thinking helps your child figure out how to respond to what she sees on Facebook.

As we've seen over the years, Facebook itself changes quite often. From a skills perspective, that's good news. Learning to adapt to change may be the most important skill for success in the future, as our old tools and practices become ineffective at solving emerging problems on local and global scales.

Identity skills

Whether you're arriving at a party late or making a keynote speech, self-presentation is an important skill. Most people don't get this right the first time. When our teens present themselves on Facebook, they probably won't always get it right either. That's where the experience of parents can help. From the Profile Pictures we post to Groups we join, we're projecting our identities on Facebook. Even the Friends we choose say something about who we are.

At some level, teens know Facebook is about identity—proclaiming who they are to the world. They may not know how to step back and see if they are projecting what they intend, or how to fix a mistake. Parents can certainly step up to coach their kids in this area.

Relationship skills

This last area may be a bit obvious, so let's make the point clear: Facebook is a great venue for practicing relationship skills.

Years ago, to improve relationship skills people would take the Dale Carnegie course or sign up for sales training. To build skills today, your teen doesn't have to take any course—they can just use Facebook. Your teen is connecting with new people and building relationships. Your teen is managing many loose ties and strengthening strong ties.

In the arena of relationships, some people are naturals, while others are just plain clumsy. Watching over your teen on Facebook can help you discern her abilities and help her learn relationship skills she hasn't mastered.

Parents in our classes and workshops rarely expect us to explain how Facebook builds life skills. Once we outline the five areas, parents see the potential. This is always welcome news. We find parents can get weary of the horror stories about kids being online, so seeing the positive side is a breath of fresh air.

 Linda Fogg Phillips Way to go Brittany! Las Vegas Rock N Roll 1/2 marathon finisher!

December 6, 2009 at 11:10am via Facebook Mobile 🔒 · Comment · Like ·

👍 Nicole Phillips and Valerie Anderson like this.

Brittany Phillips Herlean Thanks mom.

P.S. Scary picture!!!
December 6, 2009 at 12:04pm · Delete

Anjanele Phillips Degn That's awesome! Way to go :)
December 6, 2009 at 12:23pm · Delete

Brandon Phillips good good good going... u are a champ
December 6, 2009 at 5:32pm · Delete

BJ Fogg Good for you!
December 6, 2009 at 6:35pm · Delete

Amber Phillips thats myyyyyyy sister'
December 6, 2009 at 6:56pm · Delete

In my own life, I've seen my kids progress on the five skills above by using Facebook. In some cases, they learned on their own, through trial and error. In other cases, I've found ways to coach and teach. Other times when I've tried to help, my child didn't welcome the attention. Oh, well. Just like with other aspects of parenting, there's no "one size fits all."

4. Provide comfort and support

Facebook is a wonderful tool for supporting our children and publicly acknowledging their successes. In this way, it helps them build self-esteem and feel a sense of accomplishment.

Facebook can provide our children comfort as they journey through difficulties in life. In this capacity, Facebook has been a benefit beyond measure for my family and me.

In September 2008, my twenty-year-old son, Garrett, passed away suddenly and unexpectedly. It was, and continues to be, a devastating loss for my family and his friends. Thank heavens Garrett had a Facebook account that he used regularly prior to his passing. This is where he posted many photos of himself, friends, and family. It's where he expressed his thoughts and feelings, and he detailed his daily activities. Later, this is where his friends let the world know that he had passed away. And today, this is where his friends still go to post tender remembrances in an effort to heal their hearts. As you can imagine, Facebook has helped me to comfort others and to be comforted.

Our children are going to make mistakes in life and, as parents, so are we. Making mistakes is a critical part of their growth as well as ours. We need to be the eyes that look further down the road and the ears that hear the impending traffic in an effort to steer our children clear of the potholes and danger zones in their paths. Some of these hazards may just cause them a bump or a bruise. Others are deadly! Without the knowledge of the social networking road, we are limited in our ability to steer our children clear of the hazards that they will encounter.

Parent to parent, I suggest you embrace three principles in learning Facebook:

1. Jump in with both feet.
2. Ask questions.
3. Don't be afraid to make mistakes or to say "I'm sorry."

The most important position that we can have in life is not that of president or CEO. It is being a parent. Without you, your child's world would not exist as she knows it. One of my favorite sayings sums this up: "To the world you may be only one, but to one you are the world."

In order to have a positive effect on the lives of our children, we need to be at the crossroads of their lives. Some of the crossroads today are in the virtual world. We need to know these roads in order to be an effective guide for our children. I admit that I'm sometimes disgusted with the effects the online world has on our teens. This doesn't discourage me; instead, this fuels my battle to protect our children.

There is a proverb by the Dutch scholar Desiderius Erasmus that says, "In the land of the blind, the one-eyed man is king." In our work with parents, BJ and I have come across many who choose to live in the land of the blind when it comes to Facebook. This is not you. The fact that you're at the end of this book shows you are—or hope to be—part of your child's online world.

We commend you for joining the ranks of parents who care enough not only to arm themselves with knowledge but also to lock arms with each other in the battle to protect our children. We may never be as adept in the virtual world as our children, but by attempting to learn all that we can, we open our eyes for clearer vision and deeper understanding. We empower ourselves as parents.

We welcome your feedback

Did you find any errors in our book?

If you found problems, please let us know:
www.FacebookForParents.org/**improve**

What's next?

Invite us to **speak at your event**:
www.FacebookForParents.org/**talks**

Get **trusted help** using Facebook:
www.FacebookForParents.org/**help**

Watch our **video tutorials**:
www.FacebookForParents.org/**videos**

Join our **teaching team**:
www.FacebookForParents.org/**team**

Be part of our next book!

We invite you to **share your story** as a parent on Facebook. Our next book will features these experiences and insights.

www.FacebookForParents.org/**nextbook**

Acknowledgments

We have many people to thank for helping us along our path with **Facebook for Parents**.

First and foremost, we are indebted to our families. They supported us in teaching classes, traveling for workshops, and writing this book. You can imagine how much patience this required.

Next, we give a big thank you to Joe Quirk, whose editorial talents injected more life into each chapter.

Our appreciation goes out to Jeff Zittrain and Eliza Stefaniw, who helped with copy editing and reference work.

While we alone are responsible for all mistakes in the book, we have fewer of them thanks to those who proofed these pages: Derek Baird, Tory Bers, Michele Fogg, Sharon Greenstein, and Brittany Herlean.

Janice Clark of Good Studio Design was a delight to work with in creating the book's cover. Elaine Kwong of Elaine Kwong Design was a great help refining our design for the book's interior. And we thank Dennis Bills for his photo talents.

Finally, we appreciate Stanford University for being a remarkable place that allows people to explore new topics in new ways.

—Linda Fogg Phillips & BJ Fogg

JAN 1 4